HOW TO EARN $50,000+ A YEAR WITH YOUR HOME COMPUTER

Over 100 Income-Producing Projects

PHIL PHILCOX

CITADEL PRESS
Kensington Publishing Corp.
www.kensingtonbooks.com

CITADEL PRESS BOOKS are published by

Kensington Publishing Corp.
850 Third Avenue
New York, NY 10022

All Kensington titles, imprints, and distributed lines are available at special quantity discounts for bulk purchases for sales promotions, premiums, fund-raising, educational, or institutional use. Special book excerpts or customized printings can also be created to fit specific needs. For details, write or phone the office of the Kensington special sales manager: Kensington Publishing Corp., 850 Third Avenue, New York, NY 10022, attn: Special Sales Department, phone 1-800-221-2647.

Citadel Press and the Citadel Logo are trademarks of Kensington Publishing Corp.

First printing: July 2002

10 9 8 7 6 5 4 3 2 1

Printed in the United States of America

Library of Congress Control Number: 2002100676

ISBN 0-8065-2377-8

CONTENTS

Acknowledgments

I'd like to thank the following contributors for their assistance in collecting this information.

Al Bennett (http://www.bulletinboards.com/)
FunFaces.com (http://www.funfaces.com)
Gordon Internet Services (http://www.gordon-net.com)
John Soares Online Scam Report (http://onlinescamreport)
21st Century Resources
Michael McClain (http://www.astrologynumerology.com/)
Marcia Joslin, Joslin Photo Puzzle Co. (http://jigsawpuzzle.com)
John Traves Low (http://dawnstar.org/travis/portfolio/)
Cote Associates (http://www.jesup.net/cote/pubcote.htm)

INTRODUCTION

MONEYMAKING OPPORTUNITIES

Most people will agree that the computer is the invention of the century . . . this century and the last. Every day, people who never thought of owning a computer, or never even knew what a computer was, are buying them and enjoying the electronic revolution. Most are nonprofessionals, probably like yourself, home-computer users exploring the Internet, playing games, and sending e-mail to friends and family. Others use their computers for business, doing everything from running financial investment firms to designing magazines and Web pages. Considering the enormous range of things that computers can do, it's no wonder that many home computer owners are wondering what else can they do besides send e-mail and play games. *After all,* they reason, *I have a thousand dollars or more invested in this machine, so what can it do to make me some money?* The business opportunities are indeed almost unlimited, and with some determination and a few good ideas, you can turn your home computer into a moneymaker. This book is the good idea part of the equation. You have to supply the determination.

The U.S. Department of Labor recently reported that more and more people are starting to work out of their homes via computers. Those still in the workforce are communicating with their employers over the computer, working on business projects, then sending the finished products back over the Internet or telephone lines. They work on their own schedules or follow guidelines set forth by their employers. It's not uncommon to see someone working for a large corporation sitting at a computer at home dressed in pajamas.

The National Association of Home Based Businesses reports that there has been an unbelievable increase in start-up businesses in the past decade. At last count, computers were in one out of

1

every three American homes and in 88 percent of businesses. All of this is an obvious indication that computer know-how and services are in demand and will be in demand even more in the future. With small businesses making up 90 percent of the employers in this country and 70 percent of those businesses operating with staffs of less than ten, clearly they're going to need computer users like you to provide a variety of services, as well as to solve their computer problems and introduce them to new technology. After all, businesses are in business to earn a profit; many have little or no time or resources to hunt down software, turn out computer products like promotional literature, or install computer programs, learn how they operate, and use them effectively. That is the market that has opened up to home computer owners. In fact, many home computer owners themselves face similar problems, so they need help as well.

Even if your computer skills are limited, given the availability of sophisticated software and hardware, anyone (well, almost) can create products or perform services that would have been beyond their capabilities without that magic software disk or CD. When Richard D. of Pensacola, Florida discovered that his attorney's office manager was only occasionally backing up their files on disk because of the time and effort involved, he suggested they install a tape drive that would automatically back up all updated files at the end of each workday. Everything was done with a tape machine and the computer program, but the office staff were too busy to hunt down the hardware and software and install it themselves. They asked Richard to do it. Richard was just a home computer user, not a technician, but he had installed a tape drive in his own computer and knew how to do it, so he decided to give it a try.

He bought the hardware and software from a local computer shop, installed it, and programmed it for daily backups. At midnight each workday, the software turned on the tape; then the computer shifted into gear and sent all the files that had been accessed and altered that day to the tape machine. When it was done, the computer shut itself down and waited for the staff to arrive the next day and turn it on. If for some reason there was a problem the next day—the hard drive crashed or someone accidentally pushed the File Erase button—all the data was stored on the tape and recoverable. Periodically, the tape was removed and stored in a fireproof cabinet. In case of a fire, theft, or any building damage, all that data was recoverable.

For the purchase of the software and hardware, the installation, the formatting, and the time he spent teaching office workers how to use the new system, Richard was paid several hundred dollars. He discovered he had a service he could present to other businesses around town that had records, invoices, inventories, data, payrolls, and other information that was basically unprotected if the computer didn't do what it was supposed to do. To date, he's installed more than forty systems in his area and is on a retainer to update and make changes as new versions of the software are introduced.

Introducing new ideas to the marketplace is often the key to becoming a successful computer moneymaker, and this is the book that will get you started. It contains a variety of computer projects that have been tested around the country—projects you can offer with little or no experience. Many involve acting as the middle-person between a client and a provider. Others require you use your imagination, some computer skills, and a creative eye to create something other people can't create for themselves.

That's the good news. The somewhat-bad news is that with so many computer owners like you looking for a way to earn back their computer investment or supplement their income, the competition is stiff. To succeed you have to be motivated to succeed, choose the right project or projects that will work in your area, and get to it. If it requires special software, you can often download a demo version, try it out, and see if it will do the job to your satisfaction. If it does, buy it and start your business.

If you have to compete for something as simple as, say, word processing services with other computer owners looking to make money, then you have to provide a better service and product than they can, do it faster and more accurately, offer a better price, and provide them with the best product in town.

If you like teaching, there are millions of computer users out there who are baffled by how hardware and software work, so you can teach them either in your home, in their homes, or in their offices. If employees are involved, you can hold group classes and charge by the number of students. I once taught a class on how to use a spreadsheet to a group of employees at a local business and was paid $35 per employee. There were 44 employees, so I earned $35 times 44 for two evening classes, each four hours long. I made contact with some of the office managers, and they've called me in several times since to help them with other computer projects.

A woman in Los Angeles had a unique idea. Using the simple on-screen calculator that comes with Windows, she teaches children six to eight years old how to add, subtract, multiply, and divide with a calculator. On a PC using Windows, it's sitting there in the Start/Programs/Accessories group. Each session lasts fifteen minutes in Sheila's home, and she provides each child with a handheld calculator (she purchased these for less than $10) to practice at home. The whole idea was to teach kids how to use a calculator—with a computer or without. When they finished the two-week course, they were super-proficient and their parents were eager to pay Sheila for her services.

From your home or a client's home, you can teach people how to go online, send e-mail and photos, navigate the Internet, use America Online and other Internet access programs, search for stuff online, or prepare for SATs (Scholastic Aptitude Tests) and ACTs (American College Testing). Or you can give computerized music lessons; process medical forms for doctors, hospitals, and other medical services; computerize mailing lists; search family histories; and teach people how to set up an accounting system for personal or business needs. All the equipment available to do this is out there somewhere, usually in the form of software that will run on your computer. Once you teach folks, they can run everything on their own computers.

With a little artistic flair, you can design posters and business cards, flyers, newsletters, book covers, and greeting cards using a variety of font and clip art programs, all available online. Many programs include professionally laid-out templates to choose from, so you don't have to be all that inventive to design an impressive letterhead for a client. The possibilities are limited only by your imagination and the equipment available to do the job.

A twenty-five-year-old computer user in Phoenix, Arizona discovered she could design a flyer better than her local print shop staff, so she offered the printers her design services. Now the print shops get an idea of their clients' needs, then pass the design and layout job on to her via e-mail; she does the work while sitting at home. On the floor by her side is her three-year-old daughter, playing away happily. She estimates she saves about $135 a week by not requiring day-care or baby-sitting services.

She designs a couple of different layout roughs and sends them to the print shop. When (and if) the client approves, she produces the final camera-ready copy. The printer completes the job, then bills the client for the design and the printing. She gets a flat fee for each design.

If you're already in a computer-related business, you might want to offer clients some additional services and products. There are projects in this book that will fit nicely into an existing computer business. When an accountant in Montana decided that twenty-five clients were all he could handle, he offered to install accounting software on new clients' computers, configure it for their use, teach them how to use it, and act as an on-call consultant. He experimented with a few software programs that were user-friendly and found one that was fairly priced, had adequate features, and was easy to use. Now he only offers his personal accounting services to major (that is, high-paying) companies and the do-it-yourself alternative to new clients. For his consultation, the program sale, the installation and configuration, and ten hours of training for office personnel, he earns several hundred dollars per installation. If they have any problems, they call him and he responds for $50 an hour. "Responding," he said, "is an option, but the money was so good I couldn't pass it up. Most people might just want to install the software, instruct the clients, and let tech support supply them with solutions over the telephone."

If you're really computer-efficient, you can offer your services and expertise as a computer consultant. You could become the PC

Doctor, a local computer expert who will answer questions over the phone, visit the homes or offices of computer users, and generally help people solve problems. A guy in Panama City, Florida, charges $50 an hour plus travel time for home or office visits and can usually solve any hardware or software problems in an hour or so. If clients want to install a video camera for video conferencing, a new printer or scanner, some complex graphics software, or other components, he'll recommend what to buy and install it.

Last year, a doctor in his town wanted to install a modem connection to a medical database that would allow her to do research at home. She asked around, found the PC Doctor, and let him do the work. He purchased a high-speed modem and software, installed them in both her office and home computers, did the configuration, and got paid for every step of the process. When a retired colonel in my town wanted to buy a computer, he asked me what he should buy. If I was in the computer moneymaking business (instead of a writer), I could have charged him for the advice, sale, and installation. Instead, I just gave him my suggestions on what to buy and recommended a local retailer with a good reputation who could provide the equipment at a fair price; then he went out on his own. I got paid with a thank-you and a dinner at a fancy restaurant.

Obviously, you don't have to be a computer wizard to offer some of these services. Just stick with projects you think you can handle and don't get in over your head. If you're selling and installing hardware and software, stick with name brands that offer good technical support and warranties. Even the experts need advice sometimes. Buying wholesale and selling retail is an accepted practice and a good way to make money. If you can buy a software program over the Internet for 25 percent less than what you would pay at a local computer store (including shipping), you can offer it to clients and charge them full retail. With the installation of new equipment, clients might need cables, power supplies, and other accessories, so find yourself a good source of components. I've found cables that sell for $25 in local stores available by mail order over the Internet for $5. There's a list of computer accessory sources in the resource section at the end of this book.

If you're ready to make your grand entrance, you have to get your feet wet. Pick some simple projects out of this book and offer them to friends, business acquaintances, and neighbors at little or no cost. If you receive favorable responses and people start handing you money or lots of thanks, you're on your way. Now you can move up to the fee-for-services ranks. What you charge will depend on supply and demand in your area. Eventually you'll learn the art of doing business and finding clients. As your skills increase, you can adjust your rates. The more proficient you become, the more you'll be in demand.

If you prefer the peace and quiet of your home, you can work out of a spare room, communicating with clients through occasional visits, telephone, fax, modem, or e-mail contact. There are tax advantages to having your own home workplace; you can find all the details at the IRS Web site (see below). If you enjoy being with people, you can operate a business outside the home, visiting clients' offices and homes. Your choice.

If you want to seriously get into the computer moneymaking business and train for some projects, the Professional Career Development Institute offers a variety of computer-related courses you can study at home. The Web page is listed under PCDI under those subjects.

SOURCES:

IRS: http://www.irs.ustreas.gov/

GETTING STARTED—WHAT YOU'LL NEED

If you're just starting out and considering buying a computer, buy the best computer you can afford. You want as much memory as possible, and the largest hard drive, and the best motherboard you can find. Make sure there are USB connections in addition to the standard serial/parallel ports. You'll be installing programs and storing information for your own use and your clients' use, so you'll need as much hard drive space as possible. All the new pro-

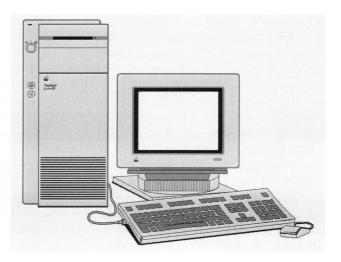

grams come on CD-ROMs, so you'll need a CD-ROM drive for downloading programs to your computer and your clients' computers. CD-ROM drives come with all current computers. You'll also need a floppy disk drive so you can copy information and provide your clients with a disk they can load into their computers.

A full-page scanner will come in handy for scanning a client's text, graphics, photos, and so forth. If you already have an older word processing program, you'll want to get the latest version of MSWord or WordPerfect, the two standards in business. Build up a collection of clip art. Corel makes a clip art collection of a million pieces on CDs and is well worth the investment. There are clip art Web sites listed elsewhere in this book.

If you already own a computer, you probably have everything you need to at least get started: the computer, a telephone, a printer, and some software. If you have a word processing program, you can provide a variety of services involving text: writing letters, transcribing, preparing manuscripts, indexing, and the like. While you can get by with the basics, you could use some additional equipment, so try to buy it now (if you can afford it). Otherwise, wait until you start earning some money.

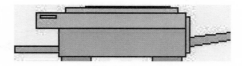

If you plan on offering services to clients at their location, a laptop computer loaded with the software you'll need to provide the service will come in handy. This will offer your clients more options (especially not having to come to your place)—and the easier you make it on your clients, the more they'll be willing to pay. Showing up at a client's home or office will earn you more money than if you e-mail them information or give advice over the telephone.

You'll need a modem (they come with all computers nowadays), Internet access, an e-mail address, and a Web page. As you read through the projects in this book, you'll find other hardware and software that you might need as well as some good sources.

Invest in a good laser jet printer. Laser jets with color are expensive, so buy a good black-and-white laser jet like the one made by HP, plus a good color ink jet printer that's relatively inexpensive (less than $100). Most of the time, you'll only be using color to show clients samples. For large print orders, color or black-and-white, you'll be using local print shops, so locate a printer in your area you can work with. A reliable printer (the live kind who runs a print shop, not the mechanical kind you plug into your computer) can not only provide you with quality printing for your clients, but also link you up with contacts in the business community who might be able to use your services. Working with a printer, when a client needs five hundred copies of a four-page color newsletter that you wrote, laid out, and designed, you get paid for the writing and editing, layout and typesetting, and the link with the printer. The printer gets the print job. Most commercial print shops can print in larger formats than 8 ½ by 14 inches—which is probably your limit—so they can print newspapers or large-format graphics like posters. Your new printer partner should offer you a

special, discounted price for bringing in the work and, if you're good, refer you to his or her clients for jobs that are outside his or her capabilities. People are always walking into print shops to get something done as well as to get help and suggestions on things other than just printing. When you find a good, reliable (and reliable is important) printer who can meet deadlines, produce good, clean printing, and is willing to pay you for your time and talent, you've found a real addition to your business, so stick with that printer. Tell your printer partner you're ready to handle any clients' needs if it's something he or she can't provide.

Many of your projects will require special papers, cards, and printing stock. Print shops have a wide assortment they can offer your clients, and working with them will give you a good assortment, but you can also stock a variety of styles, textures, and colors for simpler jobs. Parchment paper with gold seals, business card stock, certificates, and brochures with special folds are all products you can find in any office supply store or order online in bulk. There are sources for special papers and cards listed elsewhere in this book.

For home office use, a fax machine is a good investment, as is an answering machine. With a fax, you can send and receive samples or rough drafts and communicate with clients anywhere in the world—and they can respond almost immediately. A few years ago, your main means of communicating was telephone and regular mail, which was expensive and took days, often weeks to get to its destination. Now you have many options. You can use your fax machine to provide faxing services to clients and use fax software for mass faxing (the client pays the phone bill, of course). There are fax programs like Mighty Fax that work through your word processing program and computer; when linked with free (as of this writing) computer phone services, they can reduce your expenses considerably. Listing a fax number on your letterhead is some indication to would-be clients that you're well equipped to do business. With this type of equipment, your home office is essentially open twenty-four hours a day.

You'll need to have access to the Internet and an e-mail address, so sign up with AOL or a local ISP (Internet service provider). There are national ISPs that cover the entire United States, and regional ISPs (for instance, http://www.sugarriver.net/ in the Northeast, covering New Hampshire and Vermont). Working with a local ISP does have advantages if you run into problems. The only requirement is that they have a local number you can use to dial up without paying long-distance charges. Choose an ISP that offers a flat rate, not an hourly rate, and, if possible, link up with a cable provider. Unlike dial up access, which is only on when you dial up, cable access keeps you online twenty-four hours a day and allows clients to get in touch with you while you're asleep and they're wide awake somewhere else in the world. For instance, there's a six-hour difference between New York and London, so you don't want a London client instant e-mailing you at 10 A.M. her time while you're snoring away in Vermont in the early hours of the morning. Using a cable connection frees up your telephone line, which is a good idea unless you have two phone lines. You don't want local clients calling you and getting a busy signal while you're online.

Free Internet access is an option but for business purposes you need something reliable, so be prepared to pay for online access. You can probably get by with your present telephone, but two lines—one for business, one for personal use—are best. That way, you can use one to access the Internet (if you're not using cable access), freeing up the other. You can arrange to have one line with several numbers; check with your telephone provider on how to do that. Under these conditions, you can list half a dozen numbers on your letterhead and business card (sales, executive office, shipping, invoicing, and so on); when someone dials sales, for example, it rings differently than the office, shipping, and invoicing number. If you have a telephone-active family, explain that the telephone is now for both pleasure and business, so they should keep their online time to a minimum . . . or better still, install a second line or give them their own line.

Keep up with the latest developments in hardware and software. When you see something that has some business possibilities, check it out, then let your clients and local businesses know about it. Subscribe to the computer magazines, read the reviews, and keep your eyes open for new technology. When a new product comes on the market, access the company's Web page; you might even find a demo version you can play with to find out if it has some business applications you can use. When Homestead first came online with its Web page design offerings, I checked it out, found it easy to use, and now design all my Web pages with it.

SOURCES:

DialPad: http://dialpad.com
Homestead: http://homestead.com
Mighty Fax: http://mightyfax.com

FINDING CLIENTS—HOW FAR SHOULD YOU GO?

You have two basic choices when you start your computer enterprise: doing business only locally or doing business worldwide via the Internet and any other means you can to reach clients. Local business is done nose-to-nose, and while there are far fewer opportunities or profits than the other option, it's the choice of many home computer owners. It's (usually) less stressful, and you can develop a personal rapport with clients. They can reach you quickly with a phone call, and you can reach them at any time if you have any questions about the job. Having a client in Canada, Paris, or San Antonio (among other places) requires more effort, but there are also more opportunities; it's well worth considering if you're really serious about earning money with your computer. To conduct business outside your area and let people know who you are and what you do, you need a Web page and Internet connection.

For your local business, check the classified ads of your newspaper for computer-related openings. Many businesses need temporary secretaries; editors; computer operators for word processing, data processing, accounting, and bookkeeping services; and proofreaders. A recent study of 150 executives in large companies showed that 68 percent agreed that the use of temporary and offsite help would increase over the next few years. Such employees give companies flexibility in their staffing and a chance to evaluate a potential fulltime employee's capabilities. A company might need a computer operator to compile data for a new catalog—a onetime project—and if you can do the job, they can save money by hiring you as an offsite employee. Offer to do the work from home as a consultant or subcontractor, explaining your qualifications and the equipment you have available, and submitting samples of your work. As an off-site employee, there are advantages to hiring you rather than someone who comes to the office every day. For starters, you can arrange to get paid without paycheck deductions. You can do each job for a flat fee, you make your own tax arrangements, and you don't need medical insurance, paid vacations, sick leave, workers' compensation, or the use of office space and equipment. A business thinking of hiring someone would have to provide all the benefits (medical, vacation time, et cetera) and equipment necessary to do the job.

As you start earning a profit, you can put some of it back into advertising and new equipment to do new projects. If you have a few dollars to invest in your business, invest in phone calls and mailings, stuffing mailboxes with flyers, and providing samples. Word of mouth is another good way to generate business. If you provide clients with one of your products and they're pleased, ask them to tell their friends and business associates. Pass your business cards around and, above all, keep a high profile.

GETTING A WEB PAGE

Potential clients in Canada, Paris, and other places have no idea who you are and what you can do unless you reach them with your message. Your Web page (or pages) is that message sender. Once you're up and running and have a Web address, you can send it to anyone in the world via e-mail; they can take a look to see if you have something they can use. Most people have several Web pages, one for each project. When I started my freelance writing business years ago, I put many of my articles and book outlines on Web pages and invited publishers to go there to see if there was something they could use. At any given time, I have ten to fifteen Web pages, one page for each project, and they're a main source of my computer-related income. I've sold articles to magazines and newspapers all over the world via Web pages.

With a Web page online, if you're providing, for example, numerology readings or bulk e-mailing services, you can work just as easily with a client in Japan as you can with a client at the other end of your state. Using your Web page and the e-mail link between you and clients, you can communicate back and forth over the Internet almost instantly. If clients in another state or country want a numerology reading, they can provide you with whatever information you need by filling out a form you have posted on your Web page, then clicking on your e-mail link and sending it off. You'll have that information in seconds. You can provide the results via e-mail and get paid by credit card through your online account (which I'll discuss later). If clients in Tokyo want to e-mail clients in the United States with an offer, you can provide them with mailing lists and the actual e-mail sales letter.

A Web page is made up of text, images, and hyperlinks people can visit to obtain information, request your product or services, or just contact you via your e-mail address. Some ISPs offer up to five e-mail addresses per account, so you can create another e-mailbox solely for business purposes. There's a list of free e-mail address providers elsewhere in this book.

Although many computer owners use Web pages to express opinions, most people use them to do some kind of business. You can buy almost any product or service over the Internet; there are billions of sites out there. Taking a look might give you some good ideas.

There are several sources of free Web pages, and you can try them out. For business purposes, though, you'll get the best results by paying for the service. Free providers come and go, so if you choose the free route, keep trying until you find one that's easy to use and still in business. If you get a Web page from a free source and it goes out of business, all the people you've contacted with the Web page address will run into a dead end.

Your Internet access provider will give you a Web site and e-mail address, and you can post the address prominently on your Web page. All Web pages have link possibilities. Put a little icon on the page, and the viewer can click on it to get to another page or to your mailbox and send you a message.

A Web page is basically an online advertisement. People accessing your Web page are going to judge you by its appearance. If your page is graphically cluttered, unattractive, or just plain dull, you're going to have a hard time finding people to stick around to take a look at your offerings. If you're promoting your writing, proofreading, or editing services and you have some words spelled wrong, well . . . you get the idea.

Designing an attractive Web page is an art—you can use all the help you can get. Creating an original Web page from scratch requires some knowledge of HTML (hypertext markup language), a complex computer language most people can't be bothered with learning, but if you're interested there's an excellent primer on the subject at http://archive.ncsa.uiuc.edu/general/internet/www/htmlprimerall.html#hv. If you plan on designing your own Web page from scratch, I strongly suggest you go there and get familiar with the process. There are also several sites online that provide Web page templates you can download to simplify the designing process. Some include graphics. Remember, too, that most Internet service providers offer some kind of Web site services. Check and see what yours has available.

SOURCES:

Drive Thru Pickup Window: http://www.webdiner.com/templates/
Free Site Templates: http://www.freesitetemplates.com/
Netscape: http://home.netscape.com/browsers/templates/
PageKits: http://www.elated.com/pagekits/
Templates For Web Pages: http://www.wc4.org/templates.htm

FREE WEB SITE PROVIDERS:

Affinity Hosting: http://domreg.affinity.net/
AngelFire: http://angelfire.lycos.com/
The Free Pages Page: http://freepages.taronga.com/
FreeServers: http://www.thefreesite.com/Free_Web_Space/
The Free Site: http://www.thefreesite.com/Free_Web_Space/
WebSpawner: http://www.webspawner.com/
Yahoo!: http://geocities.yahoo.com/
There's a list of sites that claim to offer free Web page space for individuals and nonprofit organizations and charities at: http://members.tripod.com/~jpsp1/sites.html.

Some Web Page Design Tips

Design your page to make it clear that you have something unique and interesting to offer. The Internet allows just about everybody to step onto their own electronic soapbox and shout their message or hawk their wares to the world. As a result, there are so many pages out there—and Internet explorers are running into so much junk—that they're quickly hopping from one dull site to another.

The whole point of the Internet is to communicate. If nobody stays around long enough to explore your site and see what you have to offer, no communication is going to take place. You need to hold readers' interest and give them information on products or services they cannot find anywhere else or products or services that are better than anywhere else.

Start with a good design. Any good computer-based multimedia project begins with a good design. Your Web site should as well. The more complete your design, the better your finished product will look. You can find good designs and ideas by exploring the Internet, looking at other people's Web sites and stimulating your designing imagination. If you like the type-style on one site and the layout and graphics on another, design your site to combine the two somewhat. Just don't duplicate too much. You can right click on an online graphic and save it as a .jpeg or .bmp graphic file, but those graphics belong to someone, so ask first if you'd like to use them. Better still, go elsewhere to find a similar graphic that's in the public domain. A lot of people are very possessive about their Web page designs and won't hesitate expressing their annoyance.

When people first visit your site, they will need to know how to find their way around as quickly as possible. Your site should be well organized and have a good navigation route if it involves several pages. If people can't find what they are looking for quickly and easily, they'll get bored and start looking somewhere else.

Consider:

- How will your pages be laid out?
- What graphics will you use?
- How will your pages be linked?
- How will you position photos of some of your products?
- What are you going to say?

These details should be sketched out on paper before you begin to put things together. Plan your design so that it includes the features you like on other people's sites.

Break your site up into small units so that when people first view your page, they can skim the content quickly. For beginners, plan on putting up a one-page Web site. If you need additional space, you can add more pages later. One page will get you started so you can begin reaching out to potential clients. If and when you add more pages, stick with a common structure. This will enable visitors to find their way around without having to learn a new navigation scheme on each new page.

Check your site for what they call "link rot." The Internet is in a state of constant change. Some of the pages you link to will eventually disappear or move if they belong to someone else. One home computer owner designed a Web page that promoted his services as a book indexer. He included a link to an article that appeared in a publishing magazine about indexing and why a publisher should consider hiring a freelancer. Within a month, the article was no longer there—but the link was. Viewers of his Web page clicked but went nowhere, which they no doubt found annoying. Check the links on your site periodically to make sure they still work. Broken links make your site less appealing and unprofessional.

Not everybody on the Internet will see your graphics. Some will be browsing in text mode, so if you post a sample of one of your certificates or business cards, it could go unnoticed. Others will have automatic downloading of graphics turned off to speed things up.

Proofread your site, then view it as a visitor would. You want your site to make a good impression. Ask friends who are online to take a look and give you their comments. Do they like the colors? Do they like the layout? Is it easy to navigate? Do they get the message? Make sure there are no typographical errors, lopsided graphics, or other obvious mistakes.

A well-designed and well-built animation can enhance a Web page if it serves a good purpose, but too many of the animations on the Internet are simplistic, repetitive, and annoying. Anything that moves on your Web page will draw attention away from the static elements on the page. This means that while your visitors are trying to read your text, that bouncing ball or hopping rabbit will be distracting them.

Don't forget to include your email address and other contact information, including your mailing address and phone number. If you don't want to accept telephone calls, leave that out. All of this seems obvious, but many people forget.

Want to keep track of how many people access your Web site?

Your Web site host should be able to provide this service. If not, there are Web site access counters online that you can download.

If you can afford it, you might consider hiring a professional Web page designer. There are hundreds advertising via their Web pages on the Internet; choose someone by the appearance of his or her pages and what you can afford. If someone designs pages that appeal to you, the pages he or she designs *for* you may appeal to potential clients.

After your initial page is up and running, you can start designing additional pages for other projects. Your ISP will provide you with enough space to put up several pages.

Marketing on the Internet via a Web page isn't much different from marketing off the Internet with a full-page advertisement in a publication or a billboard on the side of the highway. You put up your message, explain what you're offering, and hope people will come into your store—wherever that is. You can offer one thing like a shoe store does, or many things like Wal-Mart does. If you have something that people need or want and hang in there, you're bound to succeed. How thoroughly you succeed will be up to you.

SOURCES:

Web Site Counter: http://www.websitedesigns.com/freecounter/

Naming Your Web Page

Most people want a Web site name that will draw attention to who they are and what they do. If you're designing logos, for instance, you might want to call your Web page thelogolady or mslogo. Unfortunately, there are millions of people ahead of you, and chances are good that any obvious Web site name is already taken. You can go to any of the Web sites listed below and enter the name you'd like to use; they'll let you know if it's available or not. If not, they might give you an alternative—say—logolady2 or 12logolady. If you can live with that, take it. There's always a fee involved with getting a domain name and posting your Web site;

that's just the cost of doing business. The Internet now has a number of suffixes, including ".com" (the most common), ".org" (used by organizations), ".edu" (for educational institutions such as universities), ".gov" (for government agencies), ".mil" (for the military), ".int" (for international), ".net" (for networks), as well as special two-letter codes assigned to countries (such as ".au" for Australia). There seems to be more and more suffixes popping up every year but, for now, ".com" is the one you will want to use for your personal or business Web site.

You can also name your Web page with your own name (something like beverlyhoskin.com or joeybananas.com). Site names like this are almost always available, but you still have to get there first.

SOURCES:

Domain Names Express: http://www.domainnamesexpress.com/main.html
Great Domains: http://www.greatdomains.com/
Register.Com: http://www.register.com/
VeriSign: http://www.netsol.com/

PROMOTING YOUR BUSINESS

Create a flyer explaining what it is you do and how people can get in touch (phone number, e-mail, or what have you), pass them around, then sit back and wait for your first client. Carry flyers around with you. Pass them out to anybody who might be a potential client and post them wherever possible. One certificate designer puts hers in clubhouses around town (VFW halls, garden clubs, and the like) and gets orders all the time. Actively promote what you plan to offer and don't hesitate to call businesses around the area and explain your computer product or services.

Create a letterhead to use for correspondence, announcements, and invoicing. Check some of the samples in the paper product catalogs listed elsewhere in this book. They have pre-designed color letterheads and business cards that are very professional looking and only need your name, address, phone number,

Web site address, and other information added before being printed out. Potential clients will judge you on your presentation, so choose wisely and don't try to design your own letterhead unless you have some experience. If clients don't like what they see in your presentation, they'll go elsewhere with their business.

Offer freebies to show people what you can do and to make connections. If the local chamber of commerce has a project coming up, design a flyer or an announcement and see if they can use it. The chamber has members who might be future clients. Contact local charities and offer them some of your work at no charge—or for your cost if it involves expenses such as printing. A bowling league might be interested in keeping club records on a computer, and there are programs on the market that do just that. You can offer one to them at cost, help them install it, and make some points in the community. One computer owner in Wisconsin said that his contributions (computerizing mailing lists and databases) to charitable organizations have resulted in contacts with several executives of local businesses and additional jobs. The contacts you make through these organizations are sources of future work, so ask about referrals and follow up on every lead. One client often leads to another. Whenever possible, sign your work with your name and phone number on the back of any printed material. This could result in additional business from someone who sees your work and wants something similar.

Once you have a Web page and an e-mail address, make sure they're printed on every piece of literature you send out. This includes your letterhead, business cards, billings to clients, sales brochures and literature, and more.

Send out news releases to local publications if you're operating only locally, and everywhere if you're doing business around the world. You can mail them by regular mail or e-mail. If you specialize in one or two areas, hunt down Web pages online with a similar theme and send them information on your new business. If you're selling wooden birdhouses over your Web page, for instance, send the news release to birding magazines, hobby magazines, woodworking magazines, and the like. If they're not interested, they can just delete your message.

Budget permitting, you can start running ads in publications. Classified ads are fairly cheap and allow you to describe what you're offering, plus include your phone number and Web page. There are thousands of people reading the newspaper who might find a use for what you're offering. A display ad is a box with words and graphics inside and differes from a classified ad, which contains words only; display ads are more expensive but much more effective.

Look around and try to find other Web pages that might be interested in linking with yours. The birdhouse builder might find a Web page devoted to ecology or hobbies that would provide a link to his site in exchange for him including a similar link. A link is a means of getting in touch with the click of a mouse. Our birdhouse builder might place a small birdhouse in the corner of the ecology-related page. The viewer clicks, and up comes the birdhouse builder's Web page. The highly commercial versions of these links are sometimes called "banner ads"; you'll see them everywhere on the Internet.

Direct mail is one of the most-often used forms of advertising. It's expensive (stamps, envelopes, and so on), but it's ideal for flyers, sales letters, and other printed material. You can compile a mailing list of potential clients in the area, design a flyer or letter, and send it off. The response rate is almost always low, but it's a start and over time could prove very effective.

Promote your business in any way possible. An article on how to build a birdhouse sent to a hobby magazine, for example, will draw attention to the birdhouse builders Web site. He can show how to build a simple birdhouse, then explain in a tag at the end that further information is available online at http://birdhouses.com.

WHAT TYPE OF BUSINESS SHOULD YOU START?

If this is your first step into the business world, you'll probably want to begin as a sole proprietorship. Business and tax rules vary around the country and many are complex, but as a sole proprietor, basically you and your business are one. All transactions are

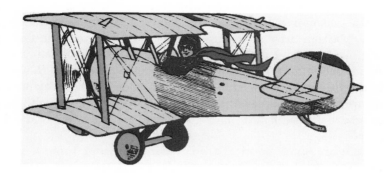

in cash or by check, and you own all the assets and pay all the bills. What's left is your profit. When you buy a ream of paper or a new computer, the cost comes out of the business, and you can deduct it from your income tax as a business expense. You'll be required to pay income taxes on your income and, in some states, collect sales tax when you bill clients. If you lose money because your business expenses exceeded your business income, you can deduct the losses from any other income you have. If you earned $35,000 last year as a schoolteacher and lost $3,000 in your home-based business, you can deduct the loss from your teaching income as long as you can prove your business is not just a hobby.

If you provide your business with a work area in your home that qualifies for a legitimate tax deduction, you can subtract a portion of your rent or mortgage, as well as utilities, repairs, and other expenses to operate and maintain your home. One computer owner in Louisiana operates his business out of one bedroom in his four-bedroom home. The bedroom is no longer a bedroom but an office, so he qualifies for deductions. He estimates that his office takes up one-fifth of the home's square footage, so he deducts one-fifth of his home operating expenses as a business expense, including insurance, repairs and improvements to that area, heating, and other expenses.

Any costs you incur while conducting your business—including travel, meals with clients, purchase of supplies, telephone calls, postage, software, Internet access, Web page design fees, and hardware—are deductible. You can hire your spouse or children, pay them a salary or commission, and deduct that as a business expense. You can drive your car while looking for clients and delivering products and deduct those expenses as well. If you think potential clients lie outside your area, you can travel, sleep in hotels, do business, even treat a client to dinner and deduct some of the expenses. If you decide to write your business name in the sky and hire a skywriter in a plane that charges $3 a word, that's deductible too.

There are some good tips on starting and operating a small business at the U.S. Small Business Administration and Onecore Web sites. If you need help or have questions, contact the Service Corps of Retired Executives; they'll hook you up with a source who can offer some free help.

SOURCES:

Onecore: http://www.oncore.com
SBA: http://www.sba.gov
SCRE: http://www.score.org

Your Home-Based Business and the IRS

The IRS is pretty clear on how you can run a business from home and deduct home business expenses from your income. The deductions for equipment and operating expenses like telephones and computers are pretty rigid; you should know what's acceptable and what isn't.

To deduct home expenses from your income, the business part of your home must be used exclusively for business and be your principal place of business—a place where you meet or deal with clients in the normal course of your business. It can also be a separate structure (not attached to your home) that you use in connection with your business. This could include an unattached garage used as a business office and nothing else.

The IRS is adamant about exclusive use. To qualify, you must use a specific area of your home only for your trade or business.

The space does not need to be marked off by a permanent partition but must be business only. For example, let's say you operate a computer business out of your den and your family uses that same den for watching TV or playing board games. Since the den is not used exclusively for business, you wouldn't be able to claim a business deduction for its use.

If you store paper, computer supplies, and other business equipment in a part of your house, you can claim expenses for that area without meeting the exclusive-use test as long as this is the only fixed location for your business, you use the space on a regular basis, and you're in the wholesale or retail selling business. An example: you operate your business out of a room that is used exclusively for your business and keep all your supplies in your basement even though your family also uses the basement for washing and drying clothes. In that case, you can deduct the expenses of the storage location.

To qualify under the trade- or business-use test, you must use part of your home in connection with a trade or business. If you use your home for a profit-seeking activity that is not a trade or business, you cannot take a deduction for its business use.

Your home office will qualify as your principal place of business for deducting expenses for its use if you meet the following requirements:

1. You use it exclusively and regularly for administrative or management activities of your trade or business.
2. You have no other fixed location where you conduct substantial administrative or management activities of your trade or business.

Alternatively, if you use your home exclusively and regularly for your business, but your home office does not qualify as your principal place of business based on the previous rules, you determine your principal place of business based on the relative importance of the activities performed at each location. If the relative importance factor does not determine your principal place of business, you can also consider the time spent at each location.

If, after considering your business locations, your home cannot be identified as your principal place of business, you cannot deduct home office expenses.

Here's a simple example: John is a home computer owner who spends most of his time at clients' homes, repairing computers. He has a small office in his home that he uses exclusively and regularly for keeping records, ordering supplies, and contacting clients. John's home office qualifies as his principal place of business for deducting expenses for its use. He has no other fixed location where he conducts these administrative or business activities. Because he meets all the qualifications, including principal place of business, he can deduct expenses (to the extent of the deduction) for the business use of his home.

The IRS has some very complicated rules on operating a home business, so check their Web site for information that might apply to your situation.

To keep track of your business, use any of the bookkeeping and accounting software programs on the market. In the long run, it will pay to install an accounting program in your computer and learn how it operates. Once you have had some experience computerizing your bookkeeping and accounting records, you can begin offering these services to others. Everybody has to deal with bookkeeping and paying taxes in one way or another, so potential clients are everywhere . . . even the neighbors next door. Clients might be interested in automating their tax records, so you can provide them with the software necessary to do the job.

You can operate your business under your own name or choose a DBA (doing business as) name. If you choose Northwest Computer Services as your DBA name, for example, there are a few simple procedures you have to follow to use the name, and these vary from state to state. This could include running an ad in the classified section of the local newspaper and filing some papers in your local courthouse. Check with the city or county licensing department. Your local zoning office can explain the rules for operating a business out of your home if you function in both modes. If you're Internet-only, you can probably get away without registering as a business—but the license cost is so small that it might be worth the investment.

Many areas prohibit home-based businesses, while others allow them with certain restrictions. One of the main objections neighbors have is customer traffic, cars parked on the street, and general disruption. If possible, avoid having clients come to your home to pick up or deliver work. If you have to make deliveries, do it. One irate neighbor calling the zoning board or homeowners' association could cancel your business. Follow some basic commonsense rules and you, your new business, and your neighbors can live in harmony.

SOFTWARE—WHO OWNS WHAT?

As a computer owner looking to earn some money, you're going to be dealing with a lot of software. You'll be buying software for your computer, suggesting that your clients buy software (or buying it for them), and providing services to a client that require you to run software on your computer or theirs.

Many software programs on the market are for owner use only, which means if you buy it, then only you can use it. If you read the lengthy fine print the software company puts on the case or in the instructions, you'll get the message. With some software, you're given a password or registration number you have to insert when you install the software; that password or number is yours exclusively. This means—if you haven't already gotten the message— that you can't buy a software program and run around town installing it on clients' computers and charging them. If you want to make a copy and give it to a friend or client so they can load it in their computer and use your registration number or password, you're breaking the law. Of course, there are exceptions, and there are software programs that anyone can use in any way they want. There are also shareware programs with no restrictions and programs that give you permission for multiple computer use.

When you purchase some of the software mentioned in this book, you can use it to perform a service or produce a product as long as the product does not conflict with the manufacturer's restrictions. For example, you can buy a word processing program and write a book or some advertising copy for a client without restrictions. You can purchase clip art and use it for a flyer if the manufacturer states there are no limitations on the use of the clip art. You can also purchase software for a client, install it on her computer and provide the client with the disk or CD, the manual, and the related paperwork. But you cannot install an accounting program on a client's computer, provide her with a copy of the manual, and then use the *same* program on another client's computer. Get the idea?

When one computer owner in Chicago bought a copy of a telephone directory on disks that could print out mailing lists by street name, zip code, and last name, he didn't realize that the content of the program he bought for $49.95 was for his use only. The information on the disk could not be provided to clients for a fee or even free. This meant that one client who asked him to prepare a mailing list of everybody who lived in three zip codes in the Chicago area couldn't get that information without the computer owner breaking the law. His only legal solution was to introduce the client to the program, explain how it worked, have her buy a copy, install it in her computer, and let her do her own zip code search. He did so and got paid for introducing the client to the software, installing it on her computer, and teaching the staff how to use it.

An interesting guide on the legal use of software is *Software Use and the Law—A Guide for Individuals, Businesses, Educational Institutions and Users Groups*. It's available from the Software Publishers Association, 1730 M Street NW, Washington, DC 20036; (202) 452-1600 (http://www.spa.org). The Business Software Alliance publishes a guide called *New Guide to Software Management* in PDF. You can download a free copy at http://www.bsa.org.

Here's the actual wording (condensed) from a software product. When you buy a software program, read the fine print closely. I've underlined the important passages:

This constitutes a legally binding contract between you and [name of company] and governs your use of the Product. By installing the product, you agree to be bound by *all of the terms and conditions stated in this agreement. If you do not wish to be bound by this agreement, you must not install or otherwise access the product.*

This agreement allows you to use the product on a nonexclusive, nontransferable, royalty-free license permitting you to download and *install the product solely for your personal use.* The rights granted to you by [name of company] shall not be assigned, sublicensed or otherwise conveyed or transferred by you to any other person, organization or entity. Any rights not expressly granted to you herein by [name of company] are reserved. You shall not decompile, reverse engineer, disassemble, or otherwise reduce the product to a human-perceivable form. *You shall not modify, sell, rent, transfer, resell, distribute, duplicate, reproduce, copy, license* or modify, or create derivative works based upon the product or any part thereof. You will not export or reexport, directly or indirectly, the product into any country prohibited by the United States Export Administration Act and the regulations thereunder.

The foregoing license gives you limited rights to use the product. You do not become the owner of the product. As between you and [name of company]. We retain all title to the product and all copies thereof. All rights not specifically granted in this agreement are reserved by [name of company]. You acknowledge and agree that [name of company] holds all rights to, title to and interest in all tangible and intangible incidents of the Product, including all patents, copyrights and trade secrets pertaining thereto, and that this agreement *conveys to you only a limited right to access and use the product.* You acknowledge that the product, including, without limitation, all code therein, contains proprietary and confidential information, are owned by [name of company] and are protected by applicable intellectual property and other laws. You shall not infringe or violate any such rights or laws. . . .

Software companies are always on the lookout for software pirates. Pirates range from ordinary, uninformed home computer owners like yourself—those who buy a copy of a computer game, load it into the computer, and then install it again in a friend's computer without knowing they're breaking the rules—to owners of warehouses filled with software duplicating equipment.

If you're in the computer moneymaking business, you'll be faced with the software dilemma some time during your moneymaking days. The most serious offenders are people who buy a software program, make multiple copies, and sell them at half price. One computer owner in California made more than five hundred copies of the computer game Myst and sold them at half price. The Software and Information Industry Association (SIIA) is the police force and can sue offenders for as much as $100,000 per title infringed. A criminal violation can mean as much as $250,000 and five years in prison.

A LESSON LEARNED

When the staff at Adirondack Disposal Services in northern California decided to upgrade their word processing program, they consulted with the brother of an employee who wasn't really an experienced computer user, but did have some personal experience with the latest version of WordPerfect. When they asked for his advice, he recommended the program, bought it for them wholesale, and spent three days trying to install it on their computer. Despite some installation problems and a clash with the ports for the printer, he finally managed to complete the job and get paid for his time and the retail price of the program. Then he left.

Unfortunately, every time someone in the office encountered a problem with the program or had difficulty making it format properly or change fonts, they called him. One problem involved aligning columns on an invoice and printing it out. This was something he had a hard time solving but after four hours of poring over the program's manual, he eventually got it straightened out. The lesson learned? Don't make guarantees and don't install software you know nothing about. Always explain to your clients the importance of filling out warranty cards and calling the software's tech support team for assistance when needed. Once you finish your work, they shouldn't be calling you for assistance unless (a) they're willing to pay you for your time, and (b) you're capable of coming up with answers. The worst thing you can say when you finish a job is, "If you have any problems, give me a call."

ACCEPTING CREDIT CARDS

A long time ago people found a need to trade. One person had something another wanted, so they traded fur pelts for horses, guns for food, and so on. Then, someone came up with a great idea called "currency." Currency represented value and allowed you to buy things without carrying the fur pelts around. Around the turn of the twentieth century, the mail-order and telephone-order businesses came along. You couldn't send currency over the telephone, and it wasn't a good idea to send cash, so we started using checks. The problem with checks is that they sometimes bounce and a lot of businesses, especially those online, don't particularly like them. When someone buys something online and

pays by check, there are always delays—and delays make for unhappy clients.

Today, we have credit cards. With a credit card, a business can get nearly instant approval, and buyers can get what they order quickly. With a credit card service on your Web page, clients can order twenty-four hours a day and you're almost assured that everything is going to go through without a problem. Credit cards are truly the currency of e-commerce; trying to do business on the Internet without the ability to accept credit cards is a bit like trying to fly a kite without wind. You're going to wear yourself out for nothing.

You need two things to accept credit cards over the Internet: a merchant account with a bank or a processing organization that will set things up for you, and a way to transfer the transaction information to the processor. This can be done by using a terminal like retail stores use—which is fine for a local transaction when your client is standing there with credit card in hand, ready to pick up the product or pay for the service. It's not workable over the Internet, however. For nose-to-nose transactions like this, the processing software you install on your desktop transmits the transactions to the processing center or an online real-time credit card processing gateway like Authorize Net, PlugNPay, Verisign, or Total Merchant Manager. Another possibility is a process-by-telephone system that allows you to transmit the transactions over a telephone keypad.

Stop a moment! All this credit card stuff is complex. Your best solution is either to use one of the credit card services available to online businesses, or to work with your bank if they make those services available.

The first step in the processing of a credit card order is to capture your client's credit card information. This can be done verbally, by mail, by fax, online by use of a shopping cart or order form, or by swiping the card in person. The way you obtain your client's credit card information is totally up to you, though you will need to specify it on your merchant account application. Once you have the credit card information, you will need to transmit it to your processing bank. The processing method you use depends on the way you take orders and the amount of money you wish to budget for the function. There are three common ways that this can be done.

One of the most common for a small Internet business is with processing software you install on your PC, such as PC Charge. The software will be configured with your merchant account number, your terminal identification number, and a specific dial-up string for the modem you have in your computer. Once your software is set up, processing a charge is simple. You simply enter the credit card information that you obtained from the client and the amount of the purchase into a window. You then send the transaction on to the processor. Your modem will dial up the processor's mainframe, usually over a toll-free number that has been configured in the software. In about five to fifteen seconds, you will see either an approval and an authorization number or a decline on your screen. The bank pays you your daily transaction total via an electronic deposit to your bank account. This is called an ACH transaction. Depending on the processing bank, it will take from two to five business days for this to occur.

If you do not want any manual tasks associated with processing, you may wish to opt for a live, real-time system like PlugNPay,

Authorize Net, Verisign, or TMM Virtual Terminal. Some of these systems contain their own shopping carts (programs to illustrate products and capture transactions), while others work in conjunction with shopping carts, applications, or systems bundled together. These systems will capture the credit card information from the Web site where the client enters it, then download it to the host server, transmit it on to the processing center, obtain the approval for (or declines) the transaction, and send a confirmation message back to the client at the site.

The disadvantages of real-time systems include the cost—you'll be charged a monthly gateway fee. Also, most systems' ability to detect and prevent fraud are good but not foolproof. Fraudulent use of credit cards at your site can result in your jeopardizing your merchant account. Credit card validity remains your responsibility, not the bank's, even though you are using an automated system. Some banks now offer their own Internet processing systems or endorse third-party systems. This could be your best choice, so check with your bank and see what programs they make available.

Another method that works well if you have only a few transactions a month is the telephone processing method. An account can be set up at a merchant bank; when you have transactions to process, you simply dial up a toll-free number and enter the transaction information over your telephone keypad. A verbal authorization follows, and the funds are automatically batched and settled. The downside to this alternative is that the rates and fees are higher than an account set up for software or terminal capture, entering a transaction takes longer and is more laborious, and there is no written documentation of authorizations and past charge history, as is the case with software or an online system. Nonetheless, this system can be an excellent alternative for your operation.

Basically, the sky is the limit when it comes to how you want to accept orders. You can take orders over the Net, by phone, by fax, walk ins, off site, trade shows—you name it. The banks consider transactions to be of two types. First, swiped transactions are those in which you actually have the credit card present and run it through a magnetic card reader or terminal. This is something you can do when you're dealing with local clients. Banks offer you a better discount rate for swiped transactions. Keyed-in transactions are any that aren't swiped. If you are selling one or a few items or services over the Internet, all you need is an interactive order form page to go with your Web site. Most services provide this, some using Form Mail installed on your hosting account as part of the package. Form Mail can make setting up your form easy without any need for programming skills. When you upload the form at your site, the client can simply fill it out, and when it is submitted, you receive the order by e-mail; a confirmation goes to the client. The form can be set up to run through a secured server (SSL) so that the information is encrypted. You'll probably find that some clients will not put their credit cards through a nonsecured server page.

Once you have the order in hand, you can use your processing software, terminal, or telephone to obtain the authorization. If you have many items or want to set up a large online store, you might need a shopping cart system like Merchant Helper. A good shopping cart will allow the client to enter an order at your site for any product you sell, selecting quantity, size, and color; obtain payment info such as credit card or check numbers; compute shipping charges and sales tax if applicable; and e-mail the order to you for processing. If you are using the shopping cart with a real-time system like TMM Virtual Terminal, the credit card has already been authorized, and you need only send the client what was ordered. Companies like 21st Century Resources now offer complete packages that provide you with everything you need to operate an online store, including your credit card merchant account, shopping cart, Web hosting account, and processing gateway system.

As a business, it's your responsibility to verify the credit card transaction. When you put through an approval and receive an authorization, that does not mean you are protected from fraud. If someone has obtained the credit card number of another person and has used it illegally, the cardholder has a right to dispute the charge. When this happens, you will receive either a merchant retrieval (an inquiry about the charge) or a chargeback. Charge-backs are something to be avoided at all costs. Excessive charge-backs can result in your account being jeopardized.

One way to deal with this is to use an address verification system (AVS). By having the address verified, you will know that you are shipping the products to the real cardholder's billing address of record, thus virtually eliminating any fraud. Features like this are included in some of the services you'll be using to accept credit cards over the Internet.

Some advice: there are a lot of companies offering credit card processing and other services. Use discretion in whom you deal with. Don't get roped into an expensive long-term lease. Don't succumb to high-pressure sales tactics. A pressure salesperson wants to get your signature before you realize how much you are overpaying.

As mentioned, this is a somewhat complicated arrangement, so you're probably going to have to pay someone for assistance and services or get some guidance from your bank. There are hundreds of companies online that advertise credit card services. They provide you with everything you need, including icon graphics you can post on your page. Clients click on a MasterCard, Visa, or American Express logo when they're ready to pay, and an application form pops up—and you've got your order.

TRADING YOUR SKILLS

When a computer owner in Illinois needed someone to install Windows and configure his computer for his new scanner and printer, he found lots of people who could do it but none he could afford. He owned a car detailing service, though, so he found a computer person who agreed to do the job in exchange for free detailing of his 1992 Corvette. A restaurant owner asked one of his customers if she knew how to install and configure his new accounting software. The customer was an ordinary home computer owner but did have some software installation experience, so they made a trade. She would install and configure the software in exchange for $200 worth of lunches and dinners. That's what you call trading.

If there are people out there who can use your services but can't afford to pay you what you think you're worth, offer to make a trade. Trading is one way to earn something for your efforts and skills without getting actual dollars in hand. That restaurant owner gave the computer owner $200 worth of lunches and dinners that actually cost him maybe $90 or so. If you trade some of your flyer design talents with a local resort and they give you a $100 room for two nights, the cost to them—if they couldn't otherwise rent the room—would be about $50 for electricity and a linen change.

Before someone invented money, everybody traded, and if they had some chickens and needed some firewood, they could probably find someone with lots of firewood but no chickens who was eager to trade.

As a start-up business, you might consider trading some of your services or products to get you started and to get some experience dealing with clients. Granted, you won't earn any money, but you can trade for things you might have bought if you had the money. If you're reading this book because you want to earn money with your home computer, limit your trading to 10 percent or less of your output and use that to trade for things you need to run your home business or things you'd otherwise buy. An office supply store can trade you for paper and toner cartridges; folks with a printer they're trying to sell might trade for some business cards or a search of their family name's history.

Note: The IRS requires that you report any trades as income. That means a $500 hotel comp you accept to compile information for a travel article must be reported as $500 in actual cash.

THE PROJECTS

All of the Web site addresses listed here are current as of press time, but time marches on; what's here today might not be here tomorrow. If you run into a dead end, you can search for the software by its name or subject. The free software entries are Web sites you can access to download free or demo copies of software related to the project.

ACCOUNTING SERVICES

Businesses and individuals keep track of their financial transactions in some organized or unorganized, sloppy, complicated, inaccurate, or unworkable manner. The unorganized are probably paying too much in taxes, not taking advantage of deductions, and, if they're in business, losing money by not collecting on accounts receivable by being generally financially disorganized. They could be your clients.

In every town, there are professional accountants eager to provide businesses and individuals with their services—but I've found that many offer more than a small business or individual needs or can afford. You can provide simple accounting services and give clients your personalized attention for a fraction of what the professionals are charging. Just don't bite off more than you can chew. You won't be doing the Wal-Mart or Sears accounts, but you can provide services to small retail stores, a restaurant or two, and a dozen or so individuals. All the work is done on your computer using accounting software.

Accounting software is available that is so simple and accurate, you can't go wrong. The client provides you with the information (just make absolutely sure it's accurate), you enter it into the pro-

gram, and out come the bottom-line figures. That's what they pay you for. You can provide them with weekly, monthly, or annual summaries and reports based on their needs and what they're willing to pay for.

A married couple, for example, might just need accounting of their expenses so they can complete their tax forms accurately at the end of the year. A small business might need some additional forms and schedules. All of this is available through the software. Most of the good accounting programs can store the records of an infinite number of clients, limited only by the amount of space on your computer. Just don't overextend yourself and take on too many clients.

"At one point," one computer owner told me, "I felt an easier option was to work with an Internet-based accounting service online that took the information I provided (provided to me by my clients), did all the processing, and sent me the end results. The finished product was very professional looking and certainly improved my status among my clients—but it was also troublesome and involved too many delays, so I decided to do it myself. Although it involved more work, I could do the same thing with a program that cost around $100."

Be careful in choosing your software package. Some are too

complex, others too simple. There are several sites on the Internet where you can download a demo version of accounting software, try it out, and, if you like it, buy it. If not, your test period will expire in a week or a month or so and there's no obligation. Some of the better programs offer online or telephone support, so if you or your client have an accounting question, you can contact them for an answer. Red Wing Accounting Software does this.

If the best chef in your town is buying his bread at Joe's Bakery and Pie Shop, you can bet that Joe's bread is likely the best in town, too. If Microsoft buys an accounting software company, you can bet that its software is some of the best available. Microsoft did just that with Great Plains Software, so check it out. It might be something you feel comfortable using. If you go to their Web site, you can download a demo version.

Find Accounting Software has a search service that will find the best accounting software based on different criteria. You can search by application, industry, operating system, developer's name, or product name. You complete an online request for a proposal; they do the rest for no charge.

SOURCES:

EasyACCT Professional Series by Intuit: http://www.taascforce.com/account/account.htm
Find Accounting: http://www.findaccountingsoftware.com
PCDI: http://www.pcdi.com
Red Wing Software: http://www.redwingsoftware.com

If you're really interested in learning the accounting business, the National Tax Training School (http://www.nattax.com/publica.htm) offers a course on operating a tax practice and a free guide to starting a tax practice.

FREE ACCOUNTING SOFTWARE:

BravoSoft: http://www.bravosoft.com
Clarisys: http://www.clarisys.ca/free.html

Great Plains Software: http://www.greatplainsquote.com
Medlin Accounting Software: http://www.medlin.com/download
.htm
Oracle Small Business: http://www.oraclesmallbusiness.com/
portal/portal.nl?mode=welcome
Quicken:http://www.cyberbounty.com/ad/?a=121&b=9999&c=
3361&offer=2

ADVERTISING DESIGN

Advertising is expensive, and a lot of businesses waste their
money with ads that just don't catch consumers' eyes or excite
them enough to purchase their product or services. Some good
examples of effective advertising can be found in major newspapers
and magazines. If companies are spending that kind of money
($35,000 a page in the *New York Times*), you can bet they're getting
a return on their investment and the advertisement is doing its
job. If you can improve on an ad you see in a local publication,
and it catches the eye of that company's decision makers, you
might find a client willing to pay you for your efforts.

We're not talking about General Motors or Disney World here.
We're talking about Joe's Air-Conditioning Shop, Stella's House of
Seafood, and/or the shoe store down the street. If they advertise,
they're spending money, and if that investment isn't bringing in a
return, then they're just throwing that money away. With a word
processing program, some clip art, and a little imagination (yours),
you might be able to produce an ad some business will like
enough to buy from you.

Look through the pages of publications in and around where
you live. When you find something you think is unimpressive, bad,
not attractive, or just clumsily worded, try to improve on it. Often
you'll find an ad in a national publication that can be modified
and sold to a local business. Just make sure you modify it enough
to stay out of trouble. Do a few samples, print them out, and send
them to the company or e-mail them as a graphics attachment.
Add a note saying you're offering it for sale. When one computer
owner in Michigan saw Harrison Clothing Store's ad in a local

newspaper with everything jammed into a one-inch by five-inch block and clip art dating back to the 1920s, she figured the Harrison people might know something about fashion but they didn't know anything about designing an ad. She reworded it, added a single photo from her clip art collection, and printed it out along with her for-sale letter. She sent it to the store manager and sold it a day later for $50. You can charge your customers what the market will bear and offer a special price on ad designs if they use some of your other services like business cards, flyer designs, or a newsletter they can mail to clients, along with mailing list maintenance. Harrison was receptive to some of these services, and the computer owner earned more than $1,000 from the store alone over a year.

ADVERTISING AGENCY ONLINE

When you design an ad layout (using your graphics program) for a client who is planning on paying a publication to run the ad, you can offer to place it in the publication and earn a commission. You get paid for the full service—the idea for an ad, the actual lay-

out, and arranging the print advertising in local publications. A computer owner in Seattle discovered that rates for display ads in local newspapers and magazines ranged from a few dollars an inch in weeklies to $750 for one-eighth of a page. By placing the advertising through her "agency," she received a 10 percent discount from the publication. She can buy a $300 ad for $270 and bill clients $300, the same amount they would pay if they did it themselves. She earns $30 plus her fee for the idea, the design, and dealing with the publication. It's an accepted practice for publications to offer this discount to agencies; in major markets, advertising agencies working with companies that spend a lot of money on advertising earn their income solely on advertising commissions like this.

THE ANONYMOUS MAILMAN

You or your clients can send e-mail anonymously using Manic-Mail. You enter the To, From, Subject, and text as you would with any e-mail, but the From block is left open for whatever entry name you want to choose. You can enter santaclaus@northpole.com,

arafat@opec.com, or whatever. The person receiving the mail be-
lieves the address listed in the From box is legitimate. There are
no provisions for addressees to reply, so if they click on Reply, it
drifts off into cyberspace somewhere. Obviously, it's not intended
for misuse or nasty comments. I've had several friends who wanted
to make a comment to a company or write their congressperson, a
newspaper, or an individual but were hesitant about putting their
real name in as the sender, so they used this method of communication. Your clients can even send a card with a graphic under the
same conditions.

SOURCES:

ManicMail: http://www.manicmail.net/

FREE ANONYMOUS E-MAIL:

Anonymous: http://anonymous.to/
OzeMail: http://www.ozemail.com.au/~geoffk/anon/anon.html
Send Fake E-Mail: http://www.sendfakemail.com/

APARTMENT RENTAL NEWSLETTER

How many people in your area rent an apartment or house? You can bet that anyone looking for a rental home is interested in finding the best place in the best location for the best price, and maybe a compatible roommate as well. With so many people having access to the Internet, many of them located right in your area, you can publish an online and a hard-copy print version of a rental newsletter. You'll want to keep the hard-copy print version small—say, a single 8 ½-inch by 11-inch sheet, printed on both sides if necessary. You can fill in any blank spaces with photos of rentals. You can offer both versions free and get paid by the people who are offering the properties for rent. You'll have to build up a paying audience at first so you can convince the property owners that paying you to advertise the availability of their apartments and rental homes is worth the investment and is as effective as running an ad in the local newspaper.

You can use simple formats like this:

Area	Description	Rent	Contact
Northwest	3BR/2B	$750	322-4590

Or you can get really descriptive, depending on how much the property owner wants to pay for the space on the page. This type of write-up would get top dollar:

> Three-bedroom/two-bath apartment on the northwest side, a short walk from Prospect Park. This apartment is four years old, has been recently painted, and has new carpeting and new kitchen appliances. Most of the buildings tenants are married couples without children. There are restaurants, two movie theaters, and shops nearby. Rent is $750 a month with a twelve-month lease required and a $500 security/damage deposit. #669—322-4590.

The #669 is your code number so you can keep track of the different offerings. Photos are optional; you can scan any photos provided by the owners and charge extra for including them. If you're charging for page space online and in the hard copy, you would

get more for a long write-up and a photo than for a short description.

You also have some options on how readers can get in touch with the property owners. The most profitable way is to put a link to your e-mail on the site so they can contact you, give you the code number, and you can pass on their names and telephone numbers to the property owners. In this case, you can earn a commission on each rental—which could produce enough income to eliminate the need for property owners to pay you for the advertising.

People also rent apartments and houses when they're on vacation, so you can expand your services and provide rental information at key vacation spots like Florida, Las Vegas, or the Bahamas. All this information is available online; you can act as the coordinator between the rental source and your readers. Most travel agents can also provide this type of information, but some might not want to get involved or waste space on their Web pages; introduce yourself to them as a vacation rental expert and provide them with information for their clients. They usually get some kind of commission on all transactions, which they can share with you.

Put an access counter on the Web site (your ISP can provide one) so you can keep track of how many people access your rental Web site every week, every month, and so on. That way you can tell potential clients how many people are turning to your site for information.

There are numerous national rental Web sites on the Internet, so search around and get some ideas for formatting your page. I found some interesting layouts at the Web sites below.

SOURCES:

CHT Apartment Rentals: http://www.chtapartments.com/
Homestead: http://www.springstreet.com/apartments/home.jhtml ?gate=rnet&popup=on
VacancyNet: http://www.vacancynet.com/
Vancouver Rentals (Canada): http://www.aptrentals.net/

AUCTION ONLINE

People love to buy and sell stuff, and if they can find a bargain, so much the better. An ordinary souvenir that sold for a few dollars might get ten times that amount from a collector. As they say, one person's junk is another person's treasure.

You can create an auction Web page following the format of other online auctions like eBay and others. Folks at eBay say they get more than two hundred thousand new items a week and hundreds of bids per minute. People post a description of their item with a photo and pay you for the space. Their e-mail address is included so potential buyers can contact them and make an offer. They can purchase the space for a week, a month, or any period of time and post as many items as they like. There is no limit what they can include; they can sell everything from automobiles to jewelry and anything in between.

If you want to tackle the typical auction format where people post a bid on an item that appears onscreen and the bids are constantly updated until the item is sold, take a look at the software available.

SOURCES:

Auction Broker: http://www.auctionbroker.com/
Auction Port: http://www.auctionport.com/auctioneer.html
AuctionShare: http://www.auctionshare.com/
Beyond Solutions: http://www.beyondsolutions.com/
Strictly Exchange: http://www.auctionhosting.com/

FREE AUCTION SOFTWARE:

Auction Riches: http://www.auctionriches.com/vadpro.html
Auction Row: http://www.auctionrow.com/
Auction Submit: http://www.auctionsubmit.com/features.htm

Author Online

If you've ever wanted to be a published author but just couldn't find editors to buy your work, you can use your word processing program, the Internet, and e-mail to reach thousands of editors with one click of the mouse. Once your have your article, poem, or book outline up and running, you can start searching for potential publishers of books, magazines, newsletters, newspapers . . . anyone looking for the written word. There are tens of thousands of publications looking for material, including many online publications like Boating World Online, The Poet's Corner, Home Repair America, and The Romance Network. Make a list of e-mail addresses, put your writing in the big block, and send it off. In all e-mails, there's a BCC (blind carbon copy) entry block. You can enter many addresses here, each separated by a comma, and when it arrives at the other end, it looks like it was sent only to the one addressee. The other addressees don't show. You can also offer this service to other would-be writers.

There's a list of U.S., college, and international newspapers and business magazines at Newspapers.com; thousands of newspaper, magazine, and book publishers, e-mail addresses, and/or Web sites at E-Mail Publisher/World Newspapers 2002–2003, my database, which is updated twice a year; and a list of magazines by subject at Yahoo.com. Just run down the lists, pick out the publications you think might be potential buyers, and send them your stuff.

SOURCES:

E-Mail Publisher: http://philcox.homestead.com/email.html
Newspapers.Com: http://www.newspapers.com
Yahoo: http:///search.yahoo.com/bin/search?p=magazines

FREE WRITING SOFTWARE:

Bangla Software: http://www.banglasoftware.com/
Dramatica Theory: http://storymind.com/dramatica/
DreamWater: http://www.dreamwater.org/art/falconspen/software.html

Bar Coding Services

Businesses with point-of-sale locations like department stores, auto supply stores, and clothing stores (among many others) can benefit by bar coding their products for quicker checkout. The old days of a $19.95 price tag dangling from a product on a paper tag, a checkout clerk entering $19.95 at the checkout counter, or making change out of a cigar box are just that . . . the old days. If the checkout people have ten items to deal with and they have to enter the amount for each item, it can take forever—and there's always the chance of error.

Almost all businesses use bar coding today. It speeds up the checkout process and increases accuracy. Bar coded tags automate the whole checkout process, and with the right software, everything is automatic. Bar coded tags or labels also speed up inventories.

There are different types of bar codes for retail sales and inventory and even books and videos. UPC-A is used to mark products that are sold at retail; the code identifies the manufacturer and product. UPC-E code is a compressed bar code for small items.

You can get an education on bar codes by visiting some of the Web sites below.

You can offer this product and service to your clients, and if they're short on funds, there are reconditioned units available on the Internet. The software available will print the code on labels and tags and read the product information with one quick scan during checkout and/or inventory.

SOURCES:

Barcode Software Center: http://www.mecsw.com/specs/upc_a.html
DK Data Sales: http://www.barcodesoftware.com/index.html
Electronic Imaging Materials: http://www.barcodelabels.com/about4_bar_coding.htm
Elfring Fonts: http://www.barcodingfonts.com/barmore.htm
ID Automation: http://www.idautomation.com/
Scale Buyer's Guide: http://www.scalebuyersguide.com/sbgprod/prod0003.shtml
UPC Symbology: http://www.barcodeisland.com/upca.phtml
WebCode GCI: http://www.webcode.com.br/

FREE SOFTWARE:

Advantage Information Products:
http://www.rightertrack.com/software.htm
BarCode 128: http://www.qualityshareware.com/viewapp asp?app=bar_coding/bar_code_128.xml
BarCode Factory: http://www.barcodefactory.com/software.html
Barcode Magic: http://www.qualityshareware.com/viewapp.asp?app=bar_coding/barcode_magic.xml

BIBLE STUDY CLASSES

A Bible study class for Sunday schools, small groups, Bible classes, homeschools, and family devotionalists is a popular educational tool that isn't offered in many areas outside church. Most of the classes on software are age-divided for beginners (three to six years of age), intermediates (seven to twelve years of age), and adults. The software takes you through the teaching process step by step, so no teaching experience is required. One computer owner in Washington, D.C., discovered that while Bible study was available at many of the churches in the city, some parents preferred private lessons for their children in the home. She installed the software on the clients' computers and visited their homes twice a week to conduct the online classes.

SOURCES:

HeavenWord: http://www.heavenword.com/
SwordSearcher: http://www.swordsearcher.com/
Theophilos: http://www.theophilos.sk/
WordSearch: http://www.wordsearchbible.com/

FREE SOFTWARE:

Bible Study Lessons: http://www.biblestudylessons.com/
Bible Study Software: http://www.seriousd.com/bible.htm
Good News Bible Study: http://www.geocities.com/lvoegtli/

Book and Report Cover Designs

You can design covers for self-published authors, book printers, company reports—anyone who needs an attractive cover. One computer owner started designing the covers for his daughter's school reports; he got so many compliments that he decided to branch out and see if he could find paying clients. One student's parent was the owner of a business that published monthly reports and distributed them to clients, and he got a steady design job, designing a different cover every month.

In some areas, there are printers who can print and bind soft-covered books for self-published book writers. Book printers differ from regular printers in that they are set up to print hundreds of book pages and bind them into something that looks like the kind of books you'd find in a bookstore. Regular printers can't really do this; when they try, the project is usually overpriced and not very professional looking because they just don't have the right equipment.

Often, writers can't get their books published by regular publishers that will pay them for their words because they're not good writers or the subjects might not be of interest, so the writers publish the books themselves. A family history book, for example, would be of no interest to the general public—but other family members might like a copy. So the writer wants a couple of dozen copies printed to pass around to family members. Some technical books have been self-published by the writers because although the content is good, there's only a limited audience for the subject. These self-published books can run from fifty to five hundred pages or more.

One problem with self-published books is the cover. Many writers choose to design their own covers, and too often it comes out looking amateurish, which can affect the sales of the book if they plan on selling it. You can offer a cover design service to writers and print shops. Before you start a job, ask the clients to go to a bookstore, find a book cover they like in design, layout, color, position of lettering, type of lettering, and so forth, and buy the book. From that book design something similar, changing it enough to avoid any copyright problems. The end result is a mas-

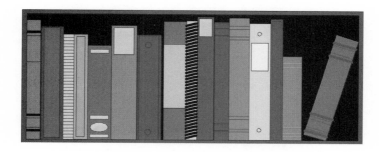

ter copy; if the clients approve, you hand it over to the printer. Because book printing projects cost thousands of dollars, a couple of hundred dollars for cover design is not unheard of. The printer can bill the client for the cover design, the majority of which goes to you.

For reports, you can work with printers and businesses in the area that regularly publish annual reports, proposals, brochures, pamphlets, and literature for distribution to their clients. Everything has to have a cover or front page attractive enough to catch someone's attention. Start collecting samples from different companies on and off the Internet, building up a collection you can refer to when you're starting a project to get your creative juices flowing.

BOOK INDEXING

According to the standard definition, an *index* is a systematic arrangement of entries designed to enable users to locate information in a document, usually a book. The process of creating an index is called indexing, and a person who does it is called an indexer.

There are many types of indexes, from cumulative indexes for journals to computer database indexes and indexes for books. In the United States, according to tradition, the index for a nonfiction book is the responsibility of the author. Most authors don't actually do it because of the work involved, so the publishers

arrange to have it done and charge the author. While a few publishers have in-house indexers, most indexing is done by freelancers, often working from home, hired by authors, publishers, or packagers. A packager is an independent business that manages the production of a book by hiring freelancers to accomplish the various tasks involved, including copyediting, proofreading, and indexing.

The indexer usually receives a set of page proofs for the book. Proofs are images of the actual pages as they will appear in the finished book, including final page numbers. The indexer reads the page proofs, making a list of headings and subheadings, the location of each reference, and the location of each reference word. For example, a book covering computer skills might have a heading for Web site construction and list it like this:

Web sites, construction of, 16, 34, 55, 67

Where the text is already on computer disk, the indexing features of word processing programs can handle the page numbers and sorting, but the real indexing work is still done by humans.

Most people interested in getting started in the indexing business send letters and resumés to publishers. You can find their addresses in *Literary Marketplace, Writer's Market, Books in Print,* and other sources.

I'm the author of forty-five nonfiction books (this is number forty-six) and have had to produce an index more than a dozen times. It's an endless task, and I'd gladly pay someone if the price was reasonable enough.

The publisher usually offers two options to writers like me: do it yourself or pay an indexer employed by the publisher. The last indexing job I paid for cost me $750, which came out of my advance. Indexing is an art, but by using the right software, you can learn how to do it and offer your services to authors and publishers. Two of the most popular are Cindex for Windows by Indexing Research and Macrex Techniques.

Cindex for Windows is available in two editions: a Standard Edition that provides features for the professional indexer, and a new Publishers' Edition that provides additional capabilities for the management of multiple projects in a networked environment. A demonstration copy of Cindex for Windows is available free at their Web site. You can also download the User's Guide in portable document format (PDF). If you are unable to download, or would like a printed copy of the User's Guide, you can buy one. The new edition features search for any text, headings, a range of indexing styles, control of page and column layout, drag-and-drop text features, spell-checking in several languages, cross-referencing, sorting by page numbers, and other useful tricks. They claim it can find any entry in 0.02 second and search through more than ten thousand text entries per second. The program runs on any IBM-compatible computer running Windows 95 or higher.

Macrex is a program designed to assist an indexer working from printed proofs, text on disk, the author's manuscript, or an already completed book. The index is created as a completely independent document that you can print out and supply your client. Version One of Macrex appeared more than twenty years ago, and the program has been under continuous development ever since. They've received a lot of input from users and have tried to make it as user-friendly as possible. All good indexing programs are complex and you'll have to devote some time to learning how to do it. Macrex has all the features of other indexing programs; you can get more information by accessing their Web pages. Additional information can be found on the Web pages of the American Society of Indexers.

SOURCES:

The American Society of Indexers: http://www.asindexing.org/
thesonet.html
Macrex Techniques: http://www.macrex.cix.co.uk/desc.htm

FREE INDEXING SOFTWARE:

Cindex for Windows: http://www.indexres.com/cindex.html
Protext: http://www.protext.com/

BOOK PROMOTION

When I wrote and self-published a book on how to move to
Florida, and where the best places are to live for different jobs, I
couldn't find any book publisher willing to publish it, even though
millions of people move to Florida every year. I created a Web
page called The Live-In Florida Page and ran some excerpts from
the book as articles, along with some Florida photos. After page
viewers read the articles, hopefully they'd be interested in learning more about the opportunity and want to buy the book. I had it
published at a print shop for $2 per copy and at the bottom of the

Web page put a photo of the book cover and information on how to order it for $10 a copy plus $2.50 postage. I created a credit card link for credit card orders and added my name and address for checks or money orders. To date, I've sold more than three hundred copies of the book. Got a book idea nobody will publish? Have some copies printed, put up a Web page, and do your own marketing. Know somebody who's self-published a book? Ask them if they'd be interested in your assisting in the marketing via the Internet.

BOOK REVIEWER

I'm an avid fiction and nonfiction book reader and, even if I do say so myself, I know a good read from a bad one. Maybe that's because for twenty years, I was an editor at a book publishing house in California. I've been writing book reviews and sending them around to publications that I think are too small or too low-budget to afford their own book reviewer. If it's a book on politics, I send it to political publications. If it's an adventure novel, I send it to men's magazines. If it's a book on boating, I send it to boating magazines. I keep my reviews down to about 500 to 750 words, putting the actual review in the e-mail and addressing it to the book review editor of the publication. If they don't have a book review editor (most don't), it goes to some other editor who can make a decision whether to buy it or delete it. There's a list of publication sources in the Author Online and other project write-ups in this book. The best list is my E-mail Publisher/World Newspapers 2002–2003: (http://philcox.homestead.com/email.html).

BOOKLET AND REPORT PRINTING

Using an ordinary word processing program, you can typeset and print booklets and reports for clients who want to produce a booklet or report to pass out information. You can do this for less than a printer will charge; for large orders, check around with print shops and find out what they charge for their printing and binding if binding is necessary.

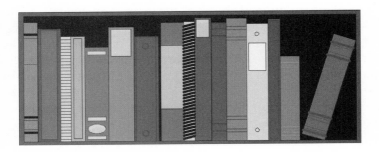

All of this—the typesetting, the printing, and the binding—is beyond the capabilities of most people, so they need a service like this. You can take a rough draft, edit it, type it in a nice type-style on the page size of their choice (eight by ten inches, five by seven inches, or the like), and print it out. If they keep the number of pages down, the pages can be folded and stapled—and out comes a booklet.

If you take a sheet of 8 ½-inch by 11-inch paper, fold it in half, fold it in half again, then open it up, you'll have you'll have four 4¼-inch by 5½-inch sections on each side. Cut the half fold and stack the paper and you'll have eight small pages. Ten sheets of ordinary twenty-pound bond paper folded and cut like this will produce eighty pages, enough for a small booklet at an expense of pennies per copy. A computer user in Vermont specializes in small booklets like this and has produced them for beauty salons (hairstyling tips), spas (health tips), and other businesses. If that size page is too small for your clients, you can fold an 8 ½-inch by 11-inch sheet in half and have four 5 ½-inch by 8 ½-inch pages, about the size of an ordinary pocketbook (give or take a few fractions of an inch).

ClickBook is a printing software program that will print any size page for brochures, greeting cards, day planners, catalogs, and booklets. You can download a free demo version from their Web site. The program takes the information, prints on both sides of the paper, and automatically rotates, reduces, and aligns the pages into the correct order so that when they're folded, they form a booklet. With ClickBook, you can also produce three-fold brochures; the program works with all of the popular word processing programs. If your printer supports double-sided printing, most good word processing programs will let you subdivide a page, select two columns and one row for the booklet format, enter the text, and print it out—the pages will come out numbered and foldable. Check your word processing program's manual to see how this is done.

Once the pages are printed and folded, you'll need a long-neck stapler to staple them together. Staple guns are available from companies like Kangaroo, Cheap Office Supplies, and Master Distributors. You might be able to find or order one from a local office supply store, or ask your printer about suppliers.

If all of this sounds like a lot of trouble, you can always edit and type the text with your word processing program, check with a local printer on having the pages printed in the format needed for a booklet, and pass the charge on to your client.

SOURCES:

Cheap Office Supplies: http://www.cheapofficesupplies.com
FinePrint Software: http://www.fineprint.com
Kangaroo: http://www.kanin.ws/
Master Distributors: http://www.masterdist.net/pfstapler/

FREE SOFTWARE:

ClickBook: http://www.bluesquirrel.com/clickBook/index.html

BULK MAILING SERVICES

Create flyers for your clients and do a bulk mailing to their potential customers in your corner of the state. If they did the mailing, they'd have to deal with the post office and pay first-class postage for each piece. If you have several clients who each mail hundreds of flyers, you can get a bulk mailing permit and pass some of the postage savings (but not all) on to your clients. That

PRSRT STD
U.S. POSTAGE
PAID
PERMIT NO.1

way, you get paid for designing and printing the flyers, affixing the mailing labels, and arranging the mailing.

The term *bulk mail* refers to quantities of mail prepared for mailing at reduced postage rates—in short, discounted first-class mail or advertising mail. In order to mail at bulk rates, you need to get a mailing permit and pay an annual mailing fee. In addition, the pieces have to be sorted by zip code. When you set up the mailing label program using your mailing software, have it print out the labels by zip codes so they're already sorted when the flyers are ready to fold or stuff envelopes. You take your bundle of mail to the post office, and off it goes. To qualify for certain postage discounts, you have to mail a minimum number of pieces, so you can combine your clients' mailings to get the best rate.

A mailing permit is permission to use a certain postage payment method for bulk and discounted mailings. There is no fee to apply for a permit to mail with precanceled stamps or a postage meter. At this writing, there is a fee for a permit to mail with a permit imprint. This onetime fee pays for setting up your permit imprint account. You must hold a permit and pay an annual mailing fee at every post office where you want to enter and pay for your mail, so you'll want to make all your mailings from the same place.

Consider offering your clients twice-a-year mailings, and find a time of year that's convenient for everyone. Most prefer February and October . . . after the big holidays and before Christmas. You can start designing the flyers at the beginning of the year, dashing back and forth between clients getting approvals, making the necessary changes, and getting ready for the printing. At this writing, you have to make a mailing at least every two years to keep the permit. The U.S. Postal Service changes rates and regulations all the time, so check with them on what the current rates and rules are.

Permit imprint is the most popular and convenient way to pay for postage, especially for high-volume mailings. Instead of using precanceled stamps or a postage meter, the permit imprint is printed in the upper right corner of the folded flyer or envelope. This is called an indicia. To use a permit imprint, you set up a postage account (called an advance deposit account) at the post office where you'll be sending the mail. When you bring your mailings to the post office, the total postage is deducted from your account.

All of your mail pieces must weigh exactly the same—and that's no problem if you're only mailing one folded 8½-inch by 11-inch piece of paper or a single sheet of paper in an envelope. Encourage your clients to use the folded flyer solution (though some might think it's too unprofessional and want envelopes). The print imprint is the best choice. You'll eliminate having to put postage on each piece, and it can be printed on a ream or more of the paper you use for your flyers or a box of No. 10 business envelopes. You can also use a rubber stamp.

SOURCES:

Bulk Mailing Software: http://www.htmlpublishing.com/html/fsww/25list/
Comco: http://www.comcoinc.com/CGIBIN/texis.exe/webinator/newsearch/
Envelope Manager: http://www.envmgr.com/home.htm
Infacta: http://www.infacta.com/gm.html
Mailing Supplies: http://www.mailingsupplies.com/mailingsoftware.htm
Mail Merry Systems: http://www.mailmerry.com/software.htm
2002 Software Pack: http://www.jbpublications.co.uk
Pragmatic: http://www.pragmaticsw.com/Pragmatic/Adbpro.htm

BULLETIN BOARDS

All businesses have a computer but only a few, especially in smaller towns, have the ability to reach out through the Internet and communicate with clients, traveling employees, satellite offices, and the general public. A bulletin board service that your business clients can use to reach out anywhere in the world could help. With a computer and an Internet connection, a satellite office anywhere in the world can communicate with the main office—regardless of location. Of course, you can also create bulletin boards for schools, nonprofit organizations, and other non-business clients.

The four businesses to which one computer owner provides bulletin boards use them mainly for traveling salespeople who are constantly dealing with clients on the road and for customer orders. Salespeople log on to the Internet from their hotels each day, access the bulletin board by typing in the URL address, and choose from a menu listing options. If they just want to send a message, they click on the mailbox with the open-door icon and write the message. To receive a message, they click on the mailbox with the closed-door icon and enter their code number. To forward an order they received that day to the accounting and shipping department, they click on the crate icon. To receive information on a product, they can choose the product line and get specs, photos, prices, and more. If they want to place an order, they can do it over the bulletin board or request a salesperson in the area to stop by and give the client the sales pitch. The main office passes all incoming messages on to the traveling salesperson. One bulletin board shows photos of each salesperson with an e-mail link under each photo.

The easiest way to provide this service is to purchase a bulletin board package (called a turnkey operation) that includes everything you need to get your clients up and running. Using your clients' computers and Internet connections, you design the board based on their requirements. You meet with the clients first, discuss what they need, make some proposals on how the board should look, show them examples and sample connection icons to install; eventually, between the two of you, you come up with some-

thing they like. Most packages include a manual on how to operate a bulletin board service, and your clients can have their bulletin board operator read up on how to do it. There are also
bulletin board service providers that take care of everything for
the client; although they're not as personal as a you-do-it, they are
an option.

Bulletin Board Software has a host bulletin board service that
charges a monthly fee. They design the board for you based on
the information you provide on their setup page. BeeBalm
Software has a demo version on their Web site that allows you to
choose bulletin board fonts and font colors, page display, background, message sorting, spell-checking, e-mail bans, and so on.
There are some sample bulletin boards at the following Web sites:

SOURCES:

Bulletin Board Software: http://www.bulletinboards.com/#top
PACorp: http://www.bulletinboards.com
Sample Bulletin Board: http://www.bulletinboards.com/
view.cfm?comcode=gdu
Sample Bulletin Board: http://www.bulletinboards.com/
view.cfm?comcode=lch93
Sample Bulletin Board: http://www.bulletinboards.com/
usermod.cfm?comcode=mch&password=642

FREE SOFTWARE:

BeeBalm: http://www.beebalm.com/
Discus: http://www.discusware.com/discus

BUMPER STICKERS

Anyone supporting a cause might be interested in having
bumper stickers printed. They can pass them out and get their
messages onto car bumpers around the area. Your clients could be
charities, politicians, musicians promoting a band—in short, people with an opinion on anything from religion to current affairs.

SOURCES:

Inkling: http://inklingsoftware.com/index.html
Iverson Software: http://www.iversonsoftware.com/success/
b2024.htm
Printing Prices: http://www.printingprices.com/main.html

BUSINESS CARDS

You can buy business card stock and software to design business cards at any office supply store. The stock comes in 8-inch by 10-inch sheets that can be separated to produce ten business cards. Everybody needs business cards, even people who aren't in business, so make some samples and show them to your friends. They might like to have something with their name, address, and phone number on it that they can hand out when someone asks them for that type of information. Offer them fifty or one hundred; for larger orders, contact a print shop to do the job.

SOURCES:

BizzCard: http://www.bizzcardcd.com/
Cam Development: http://www.camdevelopment.com/
Moss Bay Software: http://www.mossbaysoftware.com/
PrintBox: http://www.printbox.com/buscards.html
RKS Software: http://www.rkssoftware.com/vbcfaq.htm
Visual Business Card Software: http://shop.store.yahoo.com/rks/
visbuscar.html

BUSINESS LETTERS ON DISK

A recent study showed that the average business letter costs $21.45 to compose, print, and mail. Finding the right words and communicating effectively isn't always easy. You can write a variety of business letters covering different situations in MSWord, WordPerfect, or some text format that can be read by any word processing program, put them on a disk, and sell them to local businesses. A disk might contain thirty to forty different letters covering sales, a greeting to new customers, delinquent payment reminders, announcements, and more.

Each letter can contain boilerplate phrases (phrases that can be lifted and placed into almost any letter) that can be moved around using the word processing program's cut, copy, and paste features. The client can take a little bit from here and a little bit from there or use the letters as is.

An alternative to you actually writing the letters is to buy a business letter program loaded with different letters in ready-to-use format. There are also some samples you can download from the Internet, some at 4HB.com and ten sample letters you can download at Business Letters and Forms. Instant Sales Letters has a list of business letters on CD for sale, and they have a good reputation for quality.

Business Letters.Com has a collection of 240 professionally written business letters you can download in a few minutes for a small fee. The letters cover almost every business situation and are listed by category. You can provide your clients with these letters as is or modify them to cover specific situations. One computer owner said he has on occasion written a business letter for a client and e-mailed it to several customers.

SOURCES:

101 Sample Business Letters: http://www.101samplebusinessletters.com
Business Letters and Forms: http://www.businesstown.com/forms/index.asp
Business Letters.Com: http://www.businessletters.com
Instant Sales Letters: http://www.instantsalesletters.com

FREE SOFTWARE:

4HB.com: http://www.4hb.com/letters/index.html
WriteExpress: http://www.writeexpress.com/

Business Newsletters

Local businesses might be interested in publishing and distributing a newsletter they can send around to keep potential customers aware of their existence. One restaurant client of a computer owner in New Mexico publishes a one-page newsletter every month. It contains a couple of the chef's recipes, some discount coupons, some food facts, a biography of one of the employees, and photos. They give the computer owner the information and photos; he writes the copy on his word processor, scans the photos, lays everything out, and gives them a rough for their approval. If they like it, he produces a master copy and takes it to his printer. They usually order fifty to one hundred copies, so he can earn some money on the printing. He can provide the food facts by accessing the U.S. Department of Agriculture's Web site, and the clip art from any of the collections he has in his computer.

In your area, you might find an auto repair shop that would like to publish a newsletter with car-care tips and discounts for oil changes, a lawn service giving tips on lawn care, or a day-care center newsletter with tips on child care for working mothers and an invitation to take a free tour of the center.

With newsletters in hand, clients have several options. They can mail them to customers (you could supply the mailing list), distribute them from the countertop in the business, pay kids to distribute them in mailboxes, or fly over the neighborhood and drop them from an airplane (only kidding).

SOURCES:

Printing For Less: http://www.printingforless.com

Business Payroll and Check Printing

Back in the 1970s, my father owned a business that employed more than six hundred people. He once said that the hardest part of running the business was dealing with the payroll and deductions, paying taxes to the government, and keeping things in financial order. Many businesses, especially small businesses, have problems with employee payrolls, often assigning someone who has other duties to take care of payroll, too. As a result, it's easy to get things messed up—and if they get messed up enough, the government can come after them for nonpayment of required taxes.

Using any of the accounting programs on the market, you can offer businesses a computerized system that, if operated correctly, never makes a mistake. By computerizing the input information, the software makes accurate decisions, pays everybody what they're supposed to get paid after taking out deductions, and makes payroll summaries easy to access even years from now. At the end of the year, out comes the information for taxes. The information can be transferred to disk for storage and future access if necessary.

A typical program asks for a name, a Social Security number, a position title, an hourly or flat salary wage entry, a list of deductions, number of hours worked during that reporting period, and other information. It then computes what goes where and shows a bottom-line figure of that person's salary for that period. When combined with a check printing software program, it can even print out the checks, ready for signatures. Working with the personnel office, the business can supply you with information at the end of the day, week, or reporting period. This can be done by e-mail or a computer link via modem. For larger companies, it's probably best if you go there in person, install the software, show the staff how it operates, and let them make their entries when necessary.

Distinctive Software will send you an evaluation copy, and Datamatics Management Services has a free demo online.

SOURCES:

Business Electronic: http://www.payroluk.com
Comtech Solutions: http://comtechsolutions.com
Corporate Payroll Solutions: http://www.payrollsolutions.co.uk/
Optimum Solutions: http://optimumsolutions.com
Pensoft: http://www.pensoft.com/payroll.asp
Phoenix Phive: http://www.phoenixphive.com
Red Wing Accounting Software: http://www.redwingsoftware.
com/winpay.htm

FREE SOFTWARE:

Datamatics: http://www.tc1.com
Distinctive Software: http://www.distsoft.com/Eval_order.htm

SOURCES (CHECK PRINTING):

CheckPrint: http://www.checkprint.com
Check Printing Software: http://www.checkprintingsoftware.
com/tutorial/
ChequeScribe: http://www.chequescribe.com/index.html
Just Your Type: http://jyt.com/html/checksoftware.html
Performance Corporation: http://www.payformance.com/
products/
Printer People: http://www.printerpeople.com

FREE SOFTWARE (CHECK PRINTING):

Checkmate: http://www.ctechinc.com/
FinPak: http://www.finpak.com/
Payroll Companion: http://www.distsoft.com/

CAREER PLANNING SERVICES

Everybody wants the best jobs they can get and the jobs they're most suited for. Even people already in the workforce might be interested in finding out where their true talents lie and whether they should change jobs. There's career planning software available that takes clients through a series of steps and results in a computerized conclusion as to where they would find the most satisfying job and where they're most likely to succeed. The process asks them why they're in their current job, whether their true talents and abilities are really being used, and if, with some additional training, they would find a job better suited to their abilities. If clients are interested in a new career or relocating, with this information in hand, they can update their resumé (or you can update it), send it around, and see if they can find any takers. This information might be very useful to teenagers about to graduate

and enter the workforce; check with their parents and see if they're interested in having you do an analysis on their children.

SOURCES:

Career Kids:
http://www.careerkids.com/1152x864/software.html
Career Planning: http://www.bridges.com/careerplanningsoftware.htm
Discover: http://minerva.stkate.edu/offices/administrative/careerdev.nsf/pages/discover
Future42: http://www.future42.com/
Sales Search International: http://www.hotsalesjobs.com/candidate/career_planning.html

CATALOG PROVIDER

People love to thumb through catalogs, either so they can buy stuff not often available in their area or to dream about owning stuff they can't afford. It's also a great way to buy gifts that can be mailed directly to the receiver. You can provide clients with a list of free catalogs for a fee or sign them up for delivery of free catalogs. These could be special-interest catalogs (furniture and kitchen items, clothing, boating supplies, and so forth) or just a general assortment.

Searching the Internet, you'll find lots of catalogs on different subjects available directly from the manufacturer's or distributor's site. Some ask you to enter a name and address; they send the catalog by regular mail directly to your clients. Others post their catalogs online. Not everybody is on the Internet, so clients might like to get catalogs in the mail. The first step is finding a client who wants catalogs. Ask around, post flyers including your phone number in public places, check with hobby groups and friends. When you find a client who wants, for example, every catalog he or she can get, you start the hunt.

In your search engine, enter *catalogs* or a specific catalog search term like *food catalogs*. Go through each one and request that a copy be sent to your customers. Include their names, addresses and whatever other information is needed. A sample search for food catalogs brought up catalogs from Harry & David, Omaha Steaks, Betty Crocker, AKA Gourmet, the Swiss Colony, Cookie Bouquets, and more. The Betty Crocker catalog also has an online version that covers appliances, flatware, stoneware, outdoor grilling, cutlery, baking accessories, cookware, and so on, so you could provide that client with an almost endless list of catalog items.

If the catalog you're requesting is only online, you can print out a copy, assuming the cost of printing is justified. Printing only in black and white will reduce the cost considerably. If your client can afford it, make the offer. Some catalogs are only available online, so you're offering a service to people not on the Internet—something they can't get elsewhere. At CatalogLink, you can search for catalogs by name, product categories, and name brands.

SOURCES:

CatalogLine: http://www.salesmarket.com/freecatalogs.htm
CatalogLink: http://www.catalogsfreecatalogs.com/
Catalogs From A to Z: http://www.catalogsfromaz.com/
FreeWell: http://www.freewell.com/free/Free_Catalogs/
The Mall of Catalogs: http://www.mallofcatalogs.com/

CD DUPLICATION

Clients with one master CD they use to store data or as a CD catalog, or with photo CDs you create for them, might be interested in having the CD duplicated. You could do it yourself with a CD-R; that's an option for, say, up to twenty or so CDs. For mass duplication, you can work with any of the duplication services on the Internet. They can produce thousands, creating colorful inserts for the CD holders as well; you charge your clients for handling the transaction.

SOURCES:

DiscMakers: http://www.discmakers.com
HP Invent: http://www.hpcdwriter.com/products/
Plextor: http://www.plextor.com/english/products/
product_cdrw_drives.html
Yamaha: http://www.yamaha.com/cgiwin/webcgi.exe/
cHDR00007

CERTIFICATES OF ACHIEVEMENT

When people complete something that requires some effort, anything from a karate course to baby-sitting training (and everything in between), receiving a certificate of achievement is an honor. If it's fancy enough and suitable for framing, they can frame it and hang it on the wall. You can design certificates using any of the stock clip art in your graphics program or buy certificates from any of the paper sources listed in the resource section. Your clients are the course instructors who will present the certificates to graduates of their courses. Fill in the certificates with each graduate's name, add a gold seal (if you want to get fancy), and offer to supply the certificates framed. You can earn some extra

money on the framing, and chances are good the certificate will wind up on someone's wall.

CHILD INTERNET PROTECTION

Children and the Internet don't always mix well. Some Web sites are adult-oriented, and most clients with children don't want their kids going there. You can provide them with protection, using any of the software available that blocks out adult sites and sites using keywords chosen by the parent. You discuss with clients what type of information they don't want popping up on the children's computer screens, then configure the program so that that doesn't happen.

FamilyCam is a password-protected program that lets parents monitor their children's computer and online whereabouts even when they can't be with them. For each child, the client has a record log of all activity as well as snapshots of everything the child is seeing on screen regularly or randomly with settable intervals from thirty seconds to one hour; clients can also preset total usage time or limit computer access to time periods they specify. Parents can search activity logs for all programs executed, files used,

e-mail activity, every Web page hit, and length of time spent at the site.

SOURCES:

AT Kids Browser: http://www.winshare.com/
CyberSitter: http://www.solidoak.com/
FamilyCam: http://www.silverstone.net/
cmd.boa?table=Products&ID=244
MommaBear: http://www.mommabear.com/
NetNanny: http://www.netnanny.com/
ZiplogMail: http://www.ziplogmail.com/

FREE SOFTWARE:

Crayon Crawler: http://www.crayoncrawler.com/
Cyberpatrol: http://www.cyberpatrol.com/forms/homedemo.asp
SurfWatch: http://www1.surfwatch.com/

City Guidebook

If you live in an area that's popular with tourists or has a large population, you'll find people looking for information on interesting things to do, places to go, the best shopping, how to save money, and where to dine out. One computer owner wrote a sixty-page city dining-out guide using her word processing program and ClickBook and published it herself. She went to every restaurant and shop mentioned in the book and asked them if they would place half a dozen copies near the checkout register and sell them for her. They got free publicity in the book, so she figured they'd be eager to help her sell it. The book sold for $10; she paid restaurants $3 per copy sold.

This turned into an effective mutual promotional campaign and a profit maker for the computer owner. A restaurant in Manhattan sold the book, and the buyer discovered a restaurant in Brooklyn. The restaurant in Brooklyn sold the book, and the buyer discovered the restaurant in Manhattan. Everybody listed was helping promote everybody else, and the computer owner earned more than $5 per copy sold. Now she's working on a free attractions guide: fifty admission-free attractions in New York City that have interesting things going on.

FREE SOFTWARE

ClickBook: http://www.bluesquirrel.com/clickBook/index.html

COLLEGE FINANCIAL AID ADVISER

At this very moment, there are millions of high school students around the country who are concerned about their college education. Tuitions are rising at an alarming rate, and many families can't afford to send their children to college without some kind of financial aid. Most high school students discuss what type of aid is available with school counselors—but in my experience, the counselors miss out on a lot of opportunities. There are sites online that provide this type of information, as well as databases showing what type of financial assistance is available. When my neighbor's daughter was a senior about to graduate, her parents went on the Internet and found several financial assistance programs their daughter's counselor had overlooked.

There are specialized sources online for grants and funding. If your clients are interested in the biotech industry, for example, there's funding information at http://www.grantsnet.org/. You can search for grant information at http://www.grantsnet.org/. There's a list of college funding information sources and databases at: http://dir.yahoo.com/Education/Financial_Aid/ Grants/.

CollegeWhere by McCabe Software is a computerized college selection program that can provide clients with informaton on choosing a college, tell them how to write inquiry letters, and estimate the chances of gaining admission.

SOURCES:

CollegeNet: http://www.collegenet.com/about/
Financial Aid: http://www.collegeaidcounselor.com/
McCabe Software: http://mccabe.com
Scholarships/Grants: http://www.scholarships4college.com/
http://www.uwex.edu/disted/funding.html

FREE SOFTWARE:

Scholarships.Com: http://www.scholarships.com/Student_
Guide/student_guide.htm
ScholarshipSearch: http://www.fastweb.com/

CONDO NEWSLETTER

Visit local condominiums and homeowners' associations and ask the management if they'd be interested in publishing a newsletter for residents. They can use the newsletter to announce upcoming events, new rules, meetings, proposed rent or membership hikes, and other general information. There are newsletter formats on most good word processing programs with everything preformatted, so you just choose a layout and fill in the information. A newsletter can be anything from one black-and-white page to eight pages or more in color, depending on how much information is available and how much the client is willing to pay. The client pays for the cost of your services, your collection of the information, and the printing.

Somewhere in the newsletter, you can place a notice asking people to call or e-mail you so you can include the latest information in the next newsletter. You can also produce crossword puzzles

and word games relating to the area, the residents, things happening in the community, and more.

Check around to see if there are businesses that might be interested in advertising in the newsletter. This can include carpet cleaners, food delivery services, housemaid services, furniture stores, and the like. If you find advertisers, you have two choices. You can pocket the advertising money as profit or apply it to the cost of publishing the newsletter and reduce the cost to management. One computer owner published a newsletter for a homeowners' association with 165 members. The entire cost of publishing was covered by advertising, and he still earned a profit. Normally, it would cost the association $360 per issue, but he could reduce that to $150 and still make several hundred dollars' profit per issue through advertising.

Newsletters can be delivered by the management, or you can charge for delivery. One apartment complex with sixty-five apartments has the newsletter delivered by the computer owner's son, who puts a rolled-up newsletter in the door handles because you cannot stuff newsletters in mailboxes used by the U.S. Postal Service. He charged them $40 for delivery and used that to pay his son. For a teenager, $40 for an hour's work is good pay.

Contract Provider

You can offer your friends and businesses copies of any type of contract they need to conduct business or deal with a transaction. When someone sells or buys something, they should have a bill of sale. Businesses need all kinds of contracts for their everyday operations, and anyone renting property should have some kind of lease or rental agreement. On the Internet, several sites list the most common contracts; you can download them and print them out and provide them as a packet or individual forms on an as-needed basis. For an existing business client, you might want to order them a CD that contains hundreds of contracts and sell it to them or give them a copy as a thank-you for their business.

SOURCES:

Contract Forms: http://www.sampatti.com/essential_info/contract_forms.shtml
Digital Contracts: http://www.digicontracts.com/index.html
Find Forms: http://www.uslegalforms.com/findforms/closingforms.htm
Legal Documents Online: http://www.legaldocs.com/
Smart Forms: http://www.sanantoniofsbo.com/smartforms.htm
US Legal Forms: http://www.uslegalforms.com/enter.cgi?mhtext

Creative Writing Instructor

Lots of people say they'd like to be a writer, but few follow through and learn the craft. If you have some writing experience, you can start computerized writing workshops using any of the software available. Your clients might be interested in writing how-to books (this is a how-to book), fiction, poetry, or screenplays, or in learning the newspaper reporting trade. You can teach one-on-one or with small groups from around your area. You can hold classes at your home or communicate via e-mail. Students can complete assignments, sending them to you for corrections and grading. When they're finished, design a certificate with your graphics program and present one to each participant.

SOURCES:

BanglaWord: http://www.banglasoftware.com/home.html
Life Journal: http://www.lifejournal.com/
Master Freelancer: http://www.masterfreelancer.com/
wspage1.html
Novation: http://www.novalearn.com/
ScriptWriter: http://www.scriptware.com/
The Writer's Store: http://www.writersstore.com/cgibin/
SoftCart.exe/?E+writers

CREDIT CHECKING SERVICE

There are individuals and businesses in your area who might be interested in having a credit check made on someone they plan on doing business with. An apartment rental manager might want to know the status of a potential tenant, for instance. Does he have a bad credit record, or has she failed to pay for other services? The management might not want to do business with someone who might not pay a monthly rental obligation. Even if tenants sign a lease, if they're a bad risk, they're a bad risk. Employers, too, might want credit information on someone they plan to hire to see how responsible he or she is.

There are certain rules that must be followed when a credit investigation takes place. The people being investigated must sign a document saying they agree to have their credit history examined. While there are do-it-yourself options, it's best to work through an investigating service that charges you a fee, and you then charge the client that amount plus something for your services. Companies like Net Detective do just this. You download their software, provide them with the information (name, Social Security number, and so forth), and they provide you with the information.

SOURCES:

Credit FYI: http://www.creditfyi.com
Einvestigator: http://www.einvestigator.com/credit.htm
ITS Fabry: http://www.itsfabry.com/Invoicing.htm
National Credit Investigation: http://www.collectionspecialist.com/
Private Detective Online: http://www.itsfabry.com/Invoicing.htm

CROSSWORD PUZZLES

You can design custom crossword puzzles for local publications using automatic crossword-puzzle-making software. You choose a format (how many blocks up and down) and start typing in words. The program places them in the correct position. If they won't fit, some programs give you suggestions on what words to use. When the puzzle is completed, you enter the clues by typing them in. Businesses might want to sponsor a crossword they can include in local publications. A restaurant might use a puzzle with words associated with food. A medical facility might use a puzzle with words associated with health. If the publications won't use the puzzles free, the client can pay to have them published and you can arrange the payment. At the bottom of each puzzle, clients can insert a line noting their sponsorship of the puzzle—which should draw attention to their businesses.

SOURCES:

Bryson Limited: http://www.bryson.demon.co.uk/
CrossWord Challenge: http://www.pcshareware.com/dlxwordwin.htm
Crossword Compiler: http://www.crosswordcompiler.com
CrossDown for Windows: http://www.crossdown.com/AboutCrossdown.htm
CrossWorks: http://www.homeware.com/autocreate.html

FREE SOFTWARE:

Crossword Compiler: http://thinks.com/software/crosswords.htm
Free Crossword Puzzles: http://thinks.com/software/crosswords.htm

CUSTOM DIET SERVICES

People are becoming more and more health conscious, understanding that good health starts with sensible eating. People concerned about what they eat or those looking for a solution to health and weight problems can turn to you for help in choosing an effective diet. Scattered around the Internet are Web sites loaded with general diets and diets for diabetics, for people who have to watch their fat intake, and for losing weight. Most clients don't know what type of diet they should be using, so you can use a program like DietAnalyst, a free online service for determining what type of diet is best for them. You provide clients with a print-

out and some suggested recipes. Also included is information on exercise and good health.

SOURCES:

Diabetes: http://www.diabetesnet.com/software.html
FitBody: http://www.darwin326.com/fitbody/
HealthRun: http://www.healthrunr.com/main.htm
PCDI: http://www.pcdi.com
Weight Commander: http://www.weightcommander.com/

FREE SOFTWARE:

DietAid: http://www.shannonsoft.com/anonymous/dietprg.exe
DietAnalyst: http://www.dietanalyst.com
DietPower: http://www.dietpower.com/

DATA BACKUP SERVICES

How many businesses and individuals in your area back up their data and the contents of their computer in case there's a power surge, a flood, a hurricane, a tornado, or a hard disk failure?

Chances are good it's less than 50 percent, and most of those don't do it daily. According to a recent computer industry report, some do it on a now-and-then basis depending on how much time they have for backup. Forty-four percent said they never did it and just kept their fingers crossed. Only 8 percent had an automatic system that backed up everything in the computer automatically.

Studies show that average businesses have about $35,000 worth of data on their computers—which means it would cost them $35,000 to replace that data in time, research, and assistance . . . if it could be replaced. This is data that would seriously affect their business if it drifted off into cyberspace.

Most companies back up their data with tape, leave it in the computer, and do it again the next time. Tape isn't the most secure, but it is a solution. There are tens of thousands of backup tapes sitting in closets, drawers, safes, and other on-site locations, secure enough if nothing happens, possibly lost if something does.

Backing up data files is very important. Program files themselves—your word processing program, spreadsheet, Internet access, and the like—can be reinstalled if something drastic happens, but data, once it's gone, is gone for ever. An attorney I know had a hard drive failure last year and all her documents, including cases she was currently working on as well as hundreds in archive files, were completely lost. There was no way to recover any of that information.

One accountant bought a new computer; during the transfer of data, the hard disk crashed and he lost all of his records, tax forms, and client information. The office manager for a trucking firm in Kansas lost most of the company data when a power surge scrambled his hard drive. Both were clients of a backup service, however, and because the data had been backed up the night before, most of it was recoverable. One company had a computer failure that erased the information not only on the hard disk but on the tape backup as well. The horror stories go on and on.

The basic remote backup system you'll be using consists of a computer with a hard drive large enough to store gigabytes of information, a modem to connect to the client's computer, the software necessary to make the transfer, and, to be super-cautious, a tape back-up to back up the hard drive. If there are concerns as to the content of the data, encryption programs are available. If you choose this solution, you should buy a used computer that you use solely for data storage. It doesn't have to be anything fancy and shouldn't cost more than a few hundred dollars. It just has to have a modem and an extra-large hard drive.

Here's how one system works: At a preset time chosen by the user, the computer program in the client's computer scans the hard disk for any files that have been changed or added to since the last backup. All new or modified files are compressed and encrypted, ready for transmission to a host computer at your location. The encrypted files are sent via modem connection during the night to ensure that the phone lines are free and to get cheaper phone rates if long distance is involved. This is considered a better solution than sending data over the Internet, which is another option. When the data arrives at your computer, it's stored on your hard disk in the client's account file.

You can also offer to install a backup system in a client's computer, buy the necessary equipment, and get paid for sales, installation, and configuration. The easiest system to install is a tape that's attached to a port on the computer and activated by the software at a predetermined time, usually in the evening. The clients leave the computers on, set the backup time, and everything is done automatically.

SOURCES:

Creative Systems: http://www.scsidrive.com/tapebackup.htm
Consumer Depot: http://www.consumerdepot.com/categories/
tapebackup.htm
DiskOTape: http://www.disk-o-tape.com
Seagate: http://buytape.seagate.com
TMBS Computer Connections: http://www.tmbscc.com/tapes. htm_

REMOTE DATA BACKUP:

Task Force Three: http://www.bakery-net.com/rdocs/tf3/
copy.htm
TeleVault: http://www.amaonline.com/dlps/Remote.htm
ZipToNet: http://www.ziptonet.com

FREE SOFTWARE:

Backup Wolf: http://www.lonewolfsoftware.com/backupwolf.htm
FreeByte Backup: http://www.freebyte.com/fbbackup/

Data Recovery Services

Never assume that data is unrecoverable if a computer crashes. When floppies are damaged and hard drives start acting up, there are software programs and specialized companies that can at least attempt recovery of data lost due to mechanical failure, corruption, viruses, accidental erasures, power surges, and owner error. You can act as the recovery specialist in your area or as the middleperson between your clients and those companies that have the expertise to recover everything (well, almost!).

The do-it-yourself solution to data recovery is software that will perform a diagnostic routine on the ailing computer, point out the problem, and give you suggestions on how to correct it or correct it automatically. You can carry the program on CD or floppy to clients' offices and do your work there, or have them bring it to you. You can earn more if you go there.

Most of the programs available are automatic. You stick them in the computer, boot it up, click the mouse here and there, and are presented with a list of problems and suggestions on how to correct the problem. Programs like this make you look like a computer expert. Of course, there's no guarantee that you alone can solve the problem, but in many cases, the program can do the job if it's just a minor glitch the owners themselves cannot fix.

If you can correct the problem, you've earned yourself a reputation as a reliable troubleshooter. After the problem is solved, you can recommend to your clients that they buy a software program that can look ahead for problems and correct them before they have to call (and pay) you.

Several companies offer free telephone consultation to discuss a problem and give you a few tips on recovering lost data. If the problem can't be solved over the telephone, the disks or drives can be sent to companies that specialize in data recover. Depending on the extent of the damage, turnaround time is one to four days. Finances permitting, the company can even send a specialist to your area to work on clients' problems.

SOURCES:

ActionFront: http://www.actionfront.com
CBL Technologies: http://www.cbltech.com
Data Recovery Clinic: http://www.datarecoveryclinic.com
DTI Data: http://www.datarecoveryzone.com
File Recovery: http://www.filerecovery.com
Higher Ground Software: http://www.highergroundsoftware.com
Office Recovery: http://www.officerecovery.com/excel/
OnTrack: http://www.ontrack.com

Reynolds Data Recovery: http://www.datarecovery.com/main. html

Vogon: http://www.vogondatarecovery.com

FREE SOFTWARE:

ExcelRecovery: http://www.officerecovery.com/excel/

DATABASE CREATOR

Businesses with a lot of information that needs to be sorted and available by searching for keywords, inventory numbers, prices, customer address, et cetera, could use a database they can install on their computers. You can offer this service, install the database, and instruct employees on how to organize the information. If this is your first experience with database construction, buy one of the programs, play with it, and familiarize yourself with its operation. Once you become proficient, you're ready to offer your services to the unorganized. While database construction looks complex, there's a system behind every program; once you learn how to

post entries and set the sort features, you'll find them easy to use. There are some good examples of databases at Brainwave.

SOURCES:

Brainwave: http://www.brainwave.telebase.com
InstaBase: http://www.instabase.com/fproduct1.html
LodeStar: http://lodestardatabase.com/default.htm
SimpleWeb FX: http://www.simplewebfx.com/

FREE SOFTWARE:

Advantage Database: http://www.advantagedatabase.com/ADS/default.htm

DATING SERVICE ONLINE

Check out the back pages of any major city magazine like those published in New York, Atlanta, or Los Angeles, and you'll find page after page of people looking to meet other people. Subscribers to these listings usually pay per word or per line (*New York* magazine charges $30 a line) and describe themselves and the type of people they'd like to meet.

There's an opportunity here to produce a local version online or in hard copy, putting client information and photos out for others to see. You can offer the posting free and assign each person a code number. For instance, that attorney living on the west end might be M233 (M for male), or the single mom living in the suburbs might be F409 (F for female). Allowing people to post their information free should get you a lot of takers. People looking to meet other people access your page and scan the offerings. If they see someone they'd like to meet, they contact you via a link, give you the code number along with their contact payment (say, $5), and you provide them with the contact information of the person, usually an e-mail address if one is available.

E-Mail Reminder Services

Line up some clients who want to be reminded of birthdays, anniversaries, appointments, and when and where they have to be on a specific date and time, then enter their e-mail addresses in any of the reminder programs and charge them for the service.

SOURCES:

2Remember: http://calendar.stwing.upenn.edu/
All Notes: http://www.allnotes.com/
Get Reminded: http://www.getreminded.com/default.asp
Remember It: http://www.rememberit.com/
Remember To: http://www.nashville.com/~remember.to/
remember.html
Reminder Services: http://website.lineone.net/~johnfinlay/
freermnd.htm
Remind Me: http://www.gbs.com/flowers/remind.htm
Remind U-Mail: http://calendar.stwing.upenn.edu/

FREE SOFTWARE:

Condell Health Network: http://www.condell.org/wellness/
gentlereminder.html

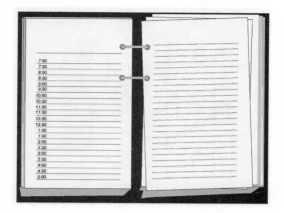

NeverForget: http://download.cnet.com/downloads/0-10021-100-897074.html
Task Plus: http://www.bizmove.com/FreeSoftware/taskplus.htm
Totally Free: http://www.totallyfreestuff.com/index.asp?ID=1061
Uremember: http://ureminder.com

EMPLOYMENT SERVICE

If your clients are interested in investigating jobs anywhere in the United States or overseas, you can find them positions in almost any location. You can search job databases by position, location, salaries, and requirements. Many have an e-mail address contact with the personnel office at the end of their write-up, so you can mail a client's resumé directly to the decision makers. You can search for jobs in any country by searching for foreign job opportunities on the Internet. There's also a job database by professional societies at http://www.careerresource.net/society/.

SOURCES:

JobBankUSA: http://www.jobbankusa.com/search.html
Job Database: http://www.uwm.edu/~ceil/career/jobs/file3.html

Job Link: http://ww.joblynx.com/
Jobs: http://www.internets.com/sjobs.htm
Monster.Com: http://monster.com

FREE SOFTWARE:

JobsAmerica: http://shareware.miningco.com/library/
homeandoffice/bl_jobsamerica.htm

EZINE PUBLISHING

An ezine is an online publication. People access the magazine's Web page and read the content. It contains photos, articles, and advertising just like a regular print magazine. As the publisher, you can put anything you want in it—the ultimate example of freedom of speech. Access is usually free, but there are people out there who will pay to express their opinions in an article, to publish a photo and caption of a product or service they're selling, or to get advertising space.

Most of the online magazines you see are ezines; look over what's available and get some ideas on publishing your own. Most computer owners publishing ezines publish something of interest to them—cooking, adult content, fishing, the martial arts, poems, or what have you.

Once you're up and running, you can start promoting the magazine by contacting people with similar interests and, most of all, potential advertisers. You can find readers by searching for Web pages related to your magazine's subject. For a cooking magazine, for example, there might be kitchen appliance stores in the area interested in buying some space, restaurants, people interested in posting their favorite menus, et cetera. There are some free ezine newsletters you can check out online to get some ideas.

SOURCES:

Free Ezine Newsletters: http://www.danexexm.dk/focalex.htm

FAMILY CRESTS AND COATS OF ARMS

If clients can provide you with a copy of their family crest or coat of arms, you can scan it into the computer, typeset some of the family's history (provided by the client or researched online), and produce a certificate suitable for framing. You can also charge for the framing service or have it matted and framed at a frame shop. If a client doesn't have a family crest but would like something to display on the wall, you can download some of the crests available in clip art programs. CorelDraw has a variety of country crests that resemble family crests. They're in the public domain, so they can be used as clients' crests, depicting the country of their families' history.

SOURCES:

Coats of Arms: http://homepage.tinet.ie/~donnaweb/
Coats of Arms: http://shop.store.yahoo.com/4crests/
CorelDraw: http://corel.com
Family Crests: http://www.familycrests.com/
Family Crests Home: http://www.scotweb.co.uk/shopping/heraldicart/

Fleur de Lis: http://www.fleurdelis.com/
Irish Surnames: http://www.irishsurnames.com/
Teleport: http://www.teleport.com/~mikenna/

FREE SOFTWARE:

Design Coat of Arms: http://www8.informatik.unierlangen.de/
html/arms.html
Free Coat of Arms: http://www.freecoatsofarms.com/
Heraldry Software: http://www.digiserve.com/heraldry/
hersoft.htm
Tartan: http://www.digiserve.com/heraldry/tartan20.zip

FLYER DESIGN, PRINTING, AND MAILING

Contact local businesses and offer to produce a flyer they can
send to potential customers, then offer to compile a mailing list
and handle all the mailings. They provide you with the information, you produce a flyer, get their okay, then have them printed in

quantity. If they need more than your printer can handle, take them to a print shop. One computer owner in New York has one client that sends out twenty-six flyers a month and another that sends out more than two hundred. If they have a mailing list, you can use it; use your computer to update any changes, then print out the labels.

Fonts

Click on Start/Settings/Control Panel/Fonts in Windows and you'll get an inventory of fonts that came with the Windows program. You can supplement your font collection for special projects and your clients' font options for their special projects by downloading any of the free fonts on the Internet or buying some of the CDs that offer a variety of fonts. There are some really neat font selections available on CD, not only in English but also in Ethiopian, Bengali, Chinese, and other foreign languages. If you're working with printers, they might be interested in updating their font collection and buying them through you. The free fonts available can be downloaded directly into any of the your clients' computers; you can get paid for traveling to their office or home, going online, and doing the job. Some of the nicest and most unique fonts I've seen anywhere are available from AGFA/ Monotype.

ACID PL   ÁÇÉĘĹŃŐŚŹŻ   KWART PL   ÁÇŔÂÓŐĹŁŻ
Arabica PL   aŔČČEĘĹŁŃŔŎ   Matura PL   AnČÇĘĘ₂ĘŅŇ₄
Arial PL   AaČĆĘĘĹŃŃÓŐŚŹŻ   OldeEnglish PL   AaŒĉŹĘŅŒĨŃ
Ae PL   AaĆĄŁĘŃŔŎŚÞŹŻŻ   OIDOMY PL   ĄĆÇŕŃŃŎÓŚŹŹŹ
Bogdad PL   AaČĆĘĘĹŃŃÁŎ óśźłźż   Paleta PL   AaĆČĆĘĘĹŃŔÓ śĺźŁ
Bohamas PL   ßąČĆĘĘĹŃŃÁŎÓŚŹŹŻ   PenArmen PL   AgĆŒĘĘₐĹŃ₄ŎŚŁź
BALON PL   ÁÇÉŃÓŚŹŻ   Penguin PL   AaČĆĘĘĹŃŃÓŐŚŹŹŻ
Barkler PL   ßąČĆĘĘĹŃŃÓŐŚŻ₄źż   Polo PL   AąČŚĘĘₐĹŃŃŎŚŁźŁ
Balki PL   AąČĆĘĘĹŃŔÓŃÓŚŹŹŻ   **PosterBodoni PL AąČĆĘĘĹ**
BOARDS PL   ĄĆŔŃÉŃĆŚŹŹŻ   Rawside PL   AąČĆŁЬÍŁÚĆŁŚźŻż
Braquart PL AąČĆĘĘĹŃŃ   Rano PL   AaŒŚĆₐŚŃŃŎŚŁźŁ
Broadalley PL AąČĆĘĘĹŃŃ   SALON PL   ĄĆĘĹŃÓŚŹŻ
BrushScript PL   AąČĆĘĘĹŃŔÓŃÓŚi   SCOTTY PL   ĄĆĘŃÓŚŹŻ
BULLETS PL ĄĆĘĹŃÓŚŻ   Scripti PL   AąČĆĘĘĹŃŃŎÓŚi
Caligraphy PL   ßąČĆĘĘĹŃŃÓŐŚŹŻ   Shadow PL   AąČĘĘĹŃŃŎÓŚŹŹŻż
Chopin PL   AąČĆĘĘĹŃ↑ÓŐŚŹ   SHADOWBOUND PL   ĄĆĘĘĹŃÓŚŻ
circles pl   ąćęńóśżż   Southon PL   ßąČĆĘĘĹŃŃŎŚżŁŻż
Cooper PL AąČĆĘĘĹŃŃÓŐŚ   Stacento PL   AąČĆĘĘĹŃŃŎŚŹźŁŻ
COTTAGE PL   ĄĆĘĹŃÓŚŹŻ   **Stressed PL AąČĆĘĘĹŃŃÓŐ**
DANA PL   ąćęńóśżł   SwissOutline PL AąČĆĘĘĹŃŃÓŐŚ
Dragon PL   ąąČŚĆₐ   SZABLON PL   ĄĆĘŃÓŚŹŻ
EDERHOUSLINE PL   ĄĆĘĘĹŃÓŚŹŻ   **SZCZHTKA PL ĄĆĘĹŃŃÓŚŹŻ**
English PL   AaČČĆĘŚₐĹÍ₄ŃₐŚ₄₃   TeamSpirit PL AąČĆĘĘĹŃŃŔÓŚŁ
FarEast PL   AąČĆĘĘĹŃŃÓŐŚŹŹŻż   Technic PL   AąČĆĘĘₐŃŃŎÓÓŚŹŹ
Fast PL   AąĆĆĘĘₐĹŃ₄Ŏ₄ŚŁ   Tempera PL   AąČĘĘĹŃŎÓŚŹ₂Ł₂₄
Hands PL   AąČĆĘĘĹŃŃÓŐŚŹŹŻż   ThirdCopy PL   AąČĆĘĘĹŃŃŎÓŚŹŹŹŻ
HomeBound PL AąČĆĘĘĹŃŃÓŐŚ   TimesNewRoman PL   AąČĆĘĘĹŃŃÓ
Karavas PL   AąČĆĘĘĹŃŃŎÓŚŹŹŻż   Vog PL   AąČĆĘĘĹŃŃÓŐŚŹŹŻ
KASIA PL   ĄČĘŃÓŚŹŻ   WildScript PL   ßąČĆĘĘₐŃŃŎŚₐŚₐ
Koala PL Bold   AąČĆₐŁŃŔŎŚₐₛŁ₃₄

SOURCES:

AFGA/Monotype: http://www.agfamonotype.co.uk
Extensis: http://www.creativeproductivitysoftware.com/font_soft
ware.htm
FontCraft: http://www.fontcraft.com/scriptorium/previews/text
previews.html
Font Expert: http://www.fontfinder.com/Software/software.html
Font Paradise: http://www.fontparadise.com
Font Software: http://wwwcgrl.cs.mcgill.ca/~luc/fontsoftware.
html
Sale On All: http://saleonall.com/cat/software/font/onesub.
html
Yahoo Shopper: http://shop.store.yahoo.com/rks/symbolselector.
html

FREE SOFTWARE:

Font Explorer: http://www.moonsoftware.com/
Free Fonts: http://www.1afreefonts.de/index2/
FreeWare Fonts: http://www.freewarefonts.com/index.html

FORMS STORE

Almost all businesses and many individuals need forms. A business uses forms for inventory, invoicing, auditing, billing, employee scheduling, and much more. Business Nation has a list of the most common forms anyone is likely to use. They're all available free online at the Web site. Depending on your clients' needs, you might find everything you need right there online. If not, you can buy software that contains all the forms most people need. One good software program can provide you with enough variety of forms to fit every business you're likely to deal with.

SOURCES:

BestForms Business Forms: http://bestforms.com
Court TV Legal Forms: http://www.courttv.com/legalhelp/business/forms/index.html
MedLaw Plus: http://www.medlawplus.com
NEBS: http://www.nebs.ca/NASApp/nebsEcat/index.jsp
SpeedFlo Business Forms: http://www.speedfloky.com
Urgent Business Forms: http://www.urgentbusinessforms.com/legal.html

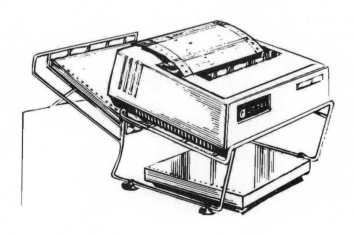

FREE SOFTWARE:

Business Nation: http://www.businessnation.com/library/forms/
Gator: http://www.gator.com/
Goverment Forms Software: http://www.enlightenedsoftware.
com/
Home Business: http://www.homebusinessonline.com/a&r/
elibrary/legal/index.shtml

Free Telephone Calls

You can provide clients with free and low-cost long-distance telephone service via the computer using any of the software and hardware available. Software like PhoneFree uses the computer's speakers and microphone and allows the user to dial any number, local or long distance, at no charge. For an additional fee, they can get low-cost connections to overseas locations. Many of the software downloads are available at no cost.

SOURCES:

InfiniSource: http://www.infinisource.com/features/
freephonecalls.html
Internet Phone: http://www.vocaltech.com
NetPhones: http://home.rochester.rr.com/netphones/
PhoneFree: http://phonefree.com

FREE WEB SITES

You can offer your clients free Web site postings if they're willing to go along with whatever restrictions the free Web page provider requires. Many put banner ads on the Web page, which could be distracting—but the page itself is free. In addition to providers of free Web sites in general, there are providers of free Web sites for nonprofit organizations, and you can find them on the Internet. Some are nationwide, some are regional, and some are dedicated to a specific area of interest (religion, medical, or the like).

SOURCES:

Creative UH Page: http://www.uhpage.com
DJ Cafe: http://members.djcafe.com
Emerald Coast: http://emerald-coast.com
Fan Space: http://www.fanspace.com
It's My Site: http://www.itsmycompany.com

FREIGHT BILL AUDITING

Unless businesses involved in shipping are keeping a close rein on expenses, they may be overpaying to move their products from one location to another. You can offer them a computerized freight bill auditing service by consulting rate guides, tariff charges, and classification sources to find the best rates available. You can do all of this at home using software and computer links with different sources over the Internet.

Once you locate overcharges or misclassifications, you can negotiate refunds for your clients and earn a percentage of the savings. The standard arrangement is 50 percent of the savings on a one-time basis or, for a regular client, 20 percent to 25 percent of the future savings resulting from your work. TrafficPro software is a Window-based auditing and payment system that automates the audit and payment of inbound and outbound truckload, parcel shipment, and airfreight bills. One home computer owner in New York City has four clients. You'll probably find the best opportuni-

ties in larger cities, although there may be local businesses that ship their products and are unaware of any overcharges. Give them a call and ask them is anyone monitoring their shipping costs.

SOURCES:

Cost Cutting Analysts: http://www.costcuttinganalysts.com/audit/freightcost.htm
TrafficPro: http://208.247.105.195/natraffic/

FUND-RAISER

With access to thousands of businesses and individuals via e-mail and through Web pages, you can offer your services as a fund-raiser for any worthy cause in your area. Create a Web page for each project and invite people in the area to take a look. On the Web page, you can explain the purpose of the fund-raising project and include an address where they can mail contributions. Check with churches, associations, charities, and other sources that have run fund-raisers before and offer your services. The standard payment for a fund-raiser is a percentage of the funds raised. You might want to consider offering something like this free of charge to organizations that could hook you up with potential clients in the future.

SOURCES:

FundEZ: http://www.fundez.com/main/mamain.htm
IMIS: http://www.advsol.com/Public/Products/iMISFR/
Non-Profit Software: http://www.npinfotech.org/tnopsi/
fundrais/frindex.htm

FREE SOFTWARE:

Ascend: http://www.ascendtech.com/
TracWorld: TracWorld: http://www.tracworld.com/

GED Tutoring

The high school dropout rate has never been higher, and most parents know that a son or daughter without a high school diploma could wind up in a dead-end career. You can offer them computerized help in guiding their children through a study program that will greatly increase their odds of passing the high school GED. There are reviews of GED software at http://www2.wgbh.org/mbcweis/ltc/alri/software.html.

SOURCES:

Aztec Software: http://www.aztecsoftware.com/
EduFax: http://www.edufax.com

Mahoney: http://www.mahoneyinteractive.com/324.htm
Merit Software: http://meritsoftware.com
PCDI: http://www.pcdi.com
Peterson's: http://www.petersons.com/testprep/ged.html
Rbizz: http://www.nbizz.com/ampm/page3.html

FREE SOFTWARE:

Ahsha Spells: http://www.jumbo.com/hobbies/files.
asp?x_fileid=173134&S=15154&ord=&mv=1\

GIFT RESEARCH AND CERTIFICATES

One computer owner told me that forty-five friends of his parents wanted to give them an anniversary gift but didn't have any unique ideas. When he found out how much they wanted to spend, he suggested they chip in and pay for a vacation in Florida and offered to help set it up. Along the Gulf Coast of Florida, he found several resort towns that were possibilities, so he searched the Internet and found an all-inclusive resort on the beach that offered accommodations and meals for one room rate, a charter boat captain advertising his services, and some information on at-

tractions. He e-mailed the resort and made reservations for four nights, then contacted the charter boat captain and arranged a day of deep-sea fishing and two tickets to a local attraction. He designed a fancy gift certificate that was presented to his parents at a dinner a couple of weeks before the event.

A few weeks later, one of their friends called the computer owner and asked him to find a gift for his brother and design a gift certificate. The brother was interested in model making, so the computer owner found a unique set of Japanese carving knives on an Internet catalog. After getting the client's okay, he ordered them, designed the certificate, and got paid for his efforts. He is now the official gift finder and certificate maker in the area. Although he has some good gift-giving ideas, it's the addition of the fancy certificate that's really of interest to clients. Often, his clients buy the gift and just have him design and print the certificate.

GROUP FLYERS

In most areas, there are dozens of places businesses can get flyers designed and printed, so sometimes you have to come up with

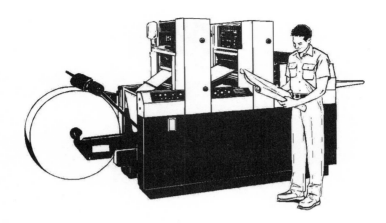

something unique that is reasonably priced and interesting enough to beat out the competition. One computer owner in Michigan designed what he calls a group flyer with two or more businesses sharing one flyer. Although he's worked with several unrelated businesses, his main clients are restaurants and take-out food establishments. Everybody likes to eat and a lot of people don't like to cook, so he offers flyer space based on what the food client wants to use (quarter page, half page, or full page). Using both sides of a flyer, he can service eight clients with quarter-page ads announcing their message. He has high school students stuff the flyers in apartment building doors (with the managers' permission, of course) so people returning home from work get the message. On one side of one flyer there might be an ad for a Chinese and pizza delivery service, a deli, and a seafood restaurant. On the other side might be a full-page announcement from a buffet restaurant in the area. You can also put together group flyers for carpet cleaners, furniture rentals, appliance repair services, and more.

HANDICAPPED COMPUTER SERVICES

Not everybody can sit down at a standard computer and get everything to operate as designed. Computers and their acces-

sories were designed for people with full functions, so users with poor eyesight, limited hand motion, and other handicaps might have problems using a computer. If they have limited hand movement, they might have problems working the keys and the mouse. Users who are totally blind can use Braille keyboards and special voice programs that read the screen and speak the words through the computer speakers. Some software programs will also take voice text spoken into the computer's microphone and convert into commands and on-screen text through a voice-activated software program.

If there are clients in your area who can use your services, you can provide them with the necessary equipment and software to accomplish everything a nonhandicapped user can do. R. J. Cooper sells keyboards with keys four times larger than regular keys. There's also a company that makes one-handed keyboards. Cooper's SwitchHopper is a switch interface that provides a place to plug switches into the computer. The switches provide standard mouse clicks and can be configured for specific keystrokes.

If you have any handicapped clients, call them up and tell them about your ability to find computer components that will simplify their lives. Windows offers some help to the handicapped in the Accessories folder. Click on it and see if there are any listed. If not, they were probably not installed when Windows was installed. You can put the Windows CD back in the computer, click on Accessories, put a check mark there—and they'll be installed. Among the tools you'll find are things that can magnify anything on the screen, high-contrast colors, and keyboard settings, including something called sticky keys. Clients might find these features useful. Speaking E-Mail by UK Software will read e-mail messages and send speaking e-mail letters.

SOURCES:

21st Century Eloquence: http://www.voicerecognition.com
Click and Type: http://www.ac.net/~lakerat/cnt/
Lernout & Hauspie: http://www.lhsl.com/default2.htm
One-Handed Keyboard Software: http://www.worklink.net/products/halfquerty.html
R. J.Cooper and Associates: http://www.rjcooper.com
Symantec: http://www.2000allsoftware.com/2000allsoftware/faxvoice.html
UK Software: http://www.uksoftware.com/speakingemail.htm
Voice-to-Text Software: http://www.zap1.com/voicetotext_home.html

HANDWRITING ANALYST

Handwriting starts in the brain; what comes out at the other end (the hand) is a key to the writer's personality. The brain not only decides what to write but how to write it using basically two types of lines—straight and curved. The brain determines how hard to press down on the writing instruments, the slant of the writing, the spacing, the size, and how fast a person writes. With the software currently available, you can offer clients an interpretation of their writing and a detailed printout report on their personality and traits.

Your clients might be business owners who want to have employees' or potential employees' handwriting analyzed to see if they're capable of handling a promotion or just people who should be hired. One computer owner's client sent him the handwriting of a woman he was dating and wanted a full report as to her true personality. Client might be folks who are curious about themselves and what their handwriting reveals. A woman client sent one handwriting analyst a copy of her great-grandmother's handwriting from the 1800s and asked her to give her an analysis of what she was really like.

SOURCES:

The ExPage: http://expage.com/page/graphoanalysis
OpenHere: http://www.openhere.com/science/psychology/
personality/handwritinganalysis/
Sheila Lowe and Associates: http://www.writinganalysis.com

FREE SOFTWARE:

Free Horoscopes: http://www.freehoroscopes.net/scripts/
horoscopeControl.asp?PAGE=handwriting
MB Handwriting Analysis: http://www.palmblvd.com/software/pc/
MBHandwritingAnalysis2000111palmpc.html
Quantum Enterprises: http://www.quantumenterprises.co.uk/
handwriting

HARD-TO-FIND STUFF FINDER

My neighbor collects salt and pepper shakers and has hundreds in her collection. She's constantly on the prowl for new additions but she's been unable to find a Mickey and Minnie Mouse set. A

search of eBay with its two and a half million listings found three sets for sale. There are numerous auction and store sites online and as a hard-to-find stuff finder, you might be able to find things other people are looking for. Announce your availability and build up a collection of Web sites that list things for sale, importers, and other sources of ordinary and unique stuff. There's a long list of auction sites listed by category online. I did a search for books I'd written more than ten years ago that have long been out of print and found six out of eight at used bookstores online.

SOURCES:

100 Top Auction Sites: http://www.100topauction.com/
Auction Sites: http://www.internetauctionlist.com/
AuctionWatch: http://www.auctionwatch.com/
BidderNetwork: http://www.biddernetwork.com/
Copernic: http://copernic.com
eBay: http://ebay.com

Hobby Collection Organizer

Folks who collect stuff as a hobby might be interested in having you come to their homes and install a computer program that will categorize and keep track of their coins, stamps, sports cards, video tapes, CDs, records, and other collectibles. Once the program is up and running, they can add new entries, remove items they've sold or traded, and compute the value of their collection. All the entries can be organized, cataloged, and sorted into categories. The inventory can be stored on disk which makes a good backup copy for insurance purposes in case of any collection damage.

SOURCES:

Accurate ID: http://5star.freeserve.com/Business/Inventory Systems/accurateidlite.html
Asset Manager: http://yippee.i4free.co.nz/html/win/homeandhobby/personalinventory.htm
Inventory Software: http://www.winappslist.com/business/inventory.htm
Stamp Organizer: http://www.winshareware.com/details.hts?f98307288
Tayden Design: http://www.tayden.com/hobby.htm

FREE SOFTWARE:

World Coins: http://www.worldcoinsexplorer.com/

Home Inspection Services

Anyone with some basic handyperson abilities or mechanical aptitude can become a computerized home or real estate inspector. Inspections are based on a visual examination of an existing structure and never involve any actual repairs or construction work, so you won't get your hands dirty. Inspectors provide clients with a computer printout analysis of the home's construction and condition, usually prior to a sale.

An average inspection takes about three hours; clients are home sellers, buyers, banks, and mortgage companies. You can market your inspection services to real estate offices, home sellers, or anyone involved in buying or selling a building or home. Reach them with an announcement of your new business by searching the Internet for their local e-mail addresses or run through the yellow pages of your telephone directory and send them a printed announcement. You can also create a home inspection Web page. You can call potential clients (get their numbers from the phone book), ask for their e-mail addresses, and send them an announcement. There are training programs available and software that will guide you through the whole process.

SOURCES:

DevWave Software: http://www.devwave.com/products/inspection.asp
Home Gauge: http://www.homegauge.com
Home Inspection 2000: http://www.homeinspection2000.com
Home Inspection Software: http://www.homeinspectionsoftware.com

InspectIt: http://www.inspectit.com
PalmTech: http://www.palm-tech.com
PCDI: http://www.pcdi.com
Sardegna: http://www.realestateinvestoronline.com/Software/
homevaluatorfacts1.htm

FREE HOME INSPECTION SOFTWARE:

Inspection Training Associates: http://www.homeinspect.com/
software/

HOME INVENTORY SERVICES

How many people, including yourself, have planned on taking
an inventory of everything in their homes in case of hurricane,
tornado, theft, or fire? Probably a lot. You can create a home inventory checklist or worksheet on your computer, visit a client's
home, walk through each room, and record each item (on paper

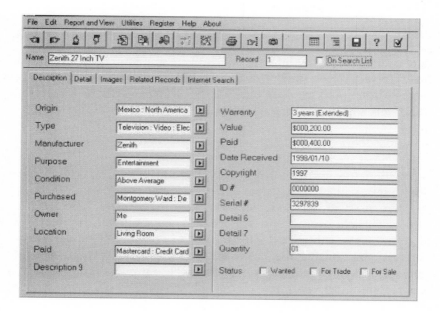

or on a tape recorder), plus, approximately when it was purchased, its value, and other information. Clients can then get a
hard copy and a copy on disk that they can store offsite in a safe
deposit box, or you can offer to keep the disks at your location.
This will keep you in touch with clients for future updates, something you can remind them of periodically.

SOURCES:

Accurate ID: http://www.accurateid.com/
I-Collect: http://www.icollect.net/
Rkom: http://www.rkom.com/inv.htm

FREE SOFTWARE:

MRTech: http://www.mrtec.com/
TrackIt: http:///www.blueocean.com/hddemo.htm

How-To Reports

If you know something other people don't know anything
about, you can write a report with your word processing program
and offer it for sale online, through advertising in newspapers and
magazines, or by e-mailing potential buyers. If you find enough
buyers, you could wind up earning more money from the report
than you would if you expanded the information and wrote a
book.

While there are no hard-and-fast rules about the length of reports, most are about fifteen hundred to two thousand words. You
store them in your word processing program; when you get an online buyer, you copy the report into an e-mail and send it off. No
postage, no printing, no hassles. One computer owner has fifteen
reports he sells over the Internet on subjects ranging from how to
communicate with your doctor to how to save money on heating
and air-conditioning the home and office. To draw attention to
the database, write articles on the subject and give them away to
related publications online, local publications, and anyone who

will take them. Make sure you include your name and Web page address.

The subjects you can write about are endless. Just pick one. What do you know something about? People are always looking for information that can save them time or money; bring them happiness; improve their relationships; make them rich; satisfy their needs for food, travel, sex, or excitement; cut their vacation costs; help them lose weight; save on the purchase of a car or house; cut their own hair; make a hundred dishes from hamburger or a chicken; and on, and on. The list is endless.

If you don't have the information for a report, you can find information everywhere. You can interview a CPA for a report on how to save on taxes; interview a travel agent for a report on budget travel; interview chefs for reports on cooking; interview military recruiters for a report on careers in the military; interview people who like to cook for a report on how to cook; talk to a mechanic on how to give your car a tune-up, or a teacher on how to teach your kids math. You can probably sell reports on how to earn money during a summer vacation, how to vacation free at popular destinations by getting a summer job, how to get a summer job in the city of your choice, or how to join the military and become a jet pilot or frogman (or woman).

A few years ago, my best-selling report was "How to Live and Work in Florida." The information was condensed from a book I was writing but never sold called *The Live-In Florida Book.* In addition to providing information about the cost of living in different areas, schools, and employment, I also included the names and addresses of more than five hundred Florida employers listed by categories such as banking, hotel/motel, sales, and the like. The book was written for people who were looking for some relief from the high unemployment and bad weather in the Northeast and Northwest. I thought it was a great idea since Florida was growing at record rates and the job opportunities were plentiful at the time, not to mention the great weather. I set up a Web page and got the word out that it was worth a visit.

Writing reports online can be a profitable computer business. There are no expenses other than your connect time and the cost of your Web page, and you can write as many reports as you want. A Web page promoting, say, ten reports on different subjects at $5 or less each, e-mailed to the buyer immediately upon payment, could prove very profitable. A report on how to get a summer job at Disney World or Disneyland might sell well if it's advertised on online and offline college newspapers.

SOURCES:

Publication Database: http://www.newsdirectory.com/.

ID CARDS

Every business of any size could use cards to identify employees. ID cards are also used in schools, clubs, and other locations that might have restricted entry. They are especially needed now in this time of heightened security. You can offer this service using ID card packages like Loronix's Instant ID. An ID card package lets you produce high-quality black-and-white or color ID cards in different formats. Instant ID comes with the software, a digital camera (or you can use your own), a plastic card printer, and the plastic card stock. Once you find a client, you arrange an ID card shoot day, set up your equipment, shoot the photos, and provide a card to each employee. When a new employee arrives, you can arrange to shoot the photo at your client's location and produce the card in your home, then mail or deliver it.

SOURCES:

Alpha Card Systems: http://www.acard.com/
Avant Photo: http://www.photoid.com/
Instant ID: http://www.instantid.com/
Photo ID: http://www.aphotoid.com/
Photo ID Systems: http://www.idbadge.com/

INCOME TAX PREPARATION

You can prepare income tax returns for individuals and very small businesses that don't want to deal with (or pay for) the more expensive tax preparers in their area. Study up on the IRS regulations and use software that does almost everything. A good tax program is Kiplinger's. You can prepare the 1040 and Schedules A, B, and C; stay away from the complex tax situations so you don't get in over your head. Most clients need only these forms. To promote your business, put together a newsletter with some tax tips you can find on the Internet and e-mail them to businesses in your area. If they think you know enough to publish a newsletter, they probably think you know enough to do their taxes. At some Web sites, you'll find free tax software downloads—some you can keep, some you can try out for a month or two.

SOURCES:

Abacus Software: http://www.abacustaxsoftware.com
ATX Forms: http://atxforms.com
H&R Block: http://www.hrblock.com
Kiplinger: http://kiplinger.com
PCDI: http://www.pcdi.com

SmallBiz Management: http://smallbizmanager.com/products/
pageSoftware.htm
Tax Software: http://taxsoftware.net/

FREE SOFTWARE:

NetCash: http://members.spree.com/business/netcash/free.html
TaxAct: http://www.taxact.com/
WorldWide Web Tax: http://www.wwwebtax.net/freetaxsoftware.
htm

JIGSAW PUZZLES

There are software programs that will take any image scanned
with a scanner and print it out in jigsaw puzzle form in sizes up to
8 ½ by 10 inches. The cardboard stock is available from the software source. Your clients might want to make a puzzle out of their
logo and offer it free to their clients as a promotional giveaway.
Parents might like to take a family photo and send it as a gift to
other family members.

You can do all of the puzzle layout with one of your graphics
programs. One computer owner told me she delivered fifty puzzles of one company's logo on a five-inch by eight-inch board with
clip art cartoons scattered around the page. They planned on giving them to their own clients' children. This is a very unique promotional idea, so it's an easy sell. Just walk into a business, show
them how it works, and chances are you'll find some clients.

SOURCES:

21st Century Jigsaw Puzzle: http://21stsoftware.com/
Jigsaw_Puzzles/
Brains Breaker: http://brainsbreaker.com
Captain's Software: http://www.unboxed.com/o/
CaptainsSoftware/
Centron Software: http://www.centronsoftware.com
CompozaPuzzle: http://www.compozapuzzle.com

Gironet: http://www.gironet.nl/home/cdon/21puzzle.htm
Jigsaws Galore: http://www.dgray.com
Mostly Wildlife: http://www.mostlywildlifephotos.com/jigsaw.htm
Photo Puzzles: http://www.jigsawpuzzle.com/products/
photo.html

FREE SOFTWARE:

21 Jigsaws: http://21stsoftware.com/Jigsaw_Puzzles/
FreeJigSaw: http://freejigsawpuzzles.com/
Java Solutions: http://javaboutique.internet.com/JSawPuzzle/
Jigsaw Puzzles: http://freebies.about.com/library/weekly/
aa070900a.htm

KOMPUTER KAMPS

"About three years ago," a computer owner in Florida told me, "I was in Cape May, New Jersey, and the hotel I was staying at was hosting a computer camp for kids. The camp supervisor had arranged for accommodations, meals, and the use of a few rooms outfitted with computers he rented from a local computer store. He had a staff of four who taught the kids the basics of computer operation. There was no complex programming or fancy stuff, and it sounded like a simple and profitable project, something I might be able to do." So when he got back to Florida, he drove down to the Keys (halfway between Miami and Key West) and found a hotel on the beach in Marathon that would provide him with rooms, meals, and the use of some conference rooms for as many kids as he could round up.

He bought six used IBM computers for $500 each and started advertising his computer camp in South Florida newspapers and on bulletin boards in schools and at supermarkets. He hired four computer-literate people who lived in Marathon and offered three-day all-inclusive camps during the school year, plus one-week camps during the summer vacation.

The camp was open to eleven- to sixteen-year-olds. He charged one price that included a shared room, three meals a day, four hours of classes daily (anything longer they found boring), and some outdoor activities like swimming, volleyball, and a half-day trip on a sailboat, which he rented along with a three-person crew. His instructors taught participants how a computer worked, how to use the Internet, how to use a word processor, how to design a Web page, and how to find anything online with search engines. During his second year, he added an advanced class that covered programming in BASIC, Visual Basic, C++, Assembler, HTML, JavaScript, and Java. His basic course is now being offered to adults who know nothing about a computer but would like to learn in a subtropical, resort-type atmosphere. His competition is a local community college with classes taught in stuffy classrooms. In other words, no competition.

On Day One, participants arrived from South Florida with their parents. He investigated the cost of renting a bus for the seventy-five-mile trip but found that most parents preferred to bring their children down and pick them up. Unescorted kids were sent down on the Greyhound bus by their parents. Over a late lunch, the group discussed the schedule and the rules, then assigned rooms; the first four-hour class was held the following morning. Classes

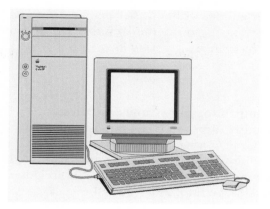

were held two hours before lunch and two hours after lunch, leaving the rest of the afternoon free. At the end of the camp, there was a graduation lunch and ceremony along with the parents, during which all participants received a fancy certificate. Then they all headed home.

You can set up a camp like this and host as few or as many participants as you think you can handle. Our computer owner in Florida suggests starting with no more than six. His first camp had four participants, and he barely earned enough to pay the instructors. But he learned from the experience—and with each camp learned something new. His last camp had twenty-four participants and turned a nice profit.

Resort areas are the best location, because you can combine classes with recreation. The best locations are within fifty to seventy-five miles of a major city so you can draw on a large urban population. That distance is also an easy commute for parents of participants. Used computers are cheap enough, and you can add to your inventory as the income comes in. At first, you can rent from someplace around the camp locale; when you start earning a profit, buy an inventory. Our Florida friend now only uses laptops, because he can transport all of them on the backseat of his car. When a camp is over, he loads up the car, settles up with the hotel/meal/room provider, pays his staff, and usually profits by several thousand dollars.

You can get an idea of how other people do it and how much they charge by logging on to the Web sites below. Note: They all carry liability insurance . . . a good idea.

SOURCES:

Computer Camp: http://www.ofmiceandkids.com
Computer Camps: http://www.computercamps.com
CyberCamps: http://www.cybercamps.com
Education Unlimited: http://www.educationunlimited.com
Future Kids: http://princetonol.com/biz/futurekids
University of Alberta: http://www.ee.ualberta.ca/~discover

LETTER AND MONOGRAM LOGOS

A variation on a graphics logo is a letter logo—a unique type-style with intertwining letters that a client can use for identification. Not unlike a monogram, the letters are more businesslike; the project is simple and easy to do. Clients can have the letter logo printed on mugs, mouse pads, baseball caps, jackets, and other products they can give away to their clients for promotional purposes. You can choose any of the fonts available from the font software listed in the Font project.

SOURCES:

Monogram Samples: http://www.wealthwood.com/crystal/
beer_stein.htm

LITERARY AGENT

A literary agent represents people who write books. There are
no qualifications required other than perserverence and the ability to reach potential publishers. One computer owner in Arizona
had a friend who wrote a book on how to make pottery. The writer
couldn't find a publisher, so the computer owner went online,
searched around, found a list of book publishers specializing in
how-to books, and e-mailed them a query. The query briefly ex-
plained the contents of the book and the writer's qualifications as
an expert. She then e-mailed the query to thirty-five publishers
and, believe it or not, got six responses asking to see more. The
writer put together a couple of sample chapters, sent them off, and,
believe it or not again, sold the book. For her services, the computer owner got 10 percent of the $2,000 advance.

If you know of any writers looking for a publisher, you can take
them on as clients, compile a database of publishers, and become
a literary agent. You can work on a commission or charge for each
query you send out. Writer's Market offers a database online that
lists publishers by subject; Yahoo has a book publisher database
you can use to look over publishers' Web sites and see what subjects they're interested in.

SOURCES:

Book and Publisher: http://www.lib.auburn.edu/acq/docs/
books.html
Book Publisher's Resources: http://www.bookpublishers.org/
Writer's Market Online: http://www.writersmarket.com/
Yahoo Book Publishers: http://search.yahoo.com/bin/
search?p=book+publishers

Logo Designing

Logos are used to identify a company and project an image. With a little practice and the right software, you can provide logos for local businesses. If you don't want to get involved in the actual designing, there are people out there who will do the design for you and your clients; you can act as the middle-person and get paid for your services.

Professional designers who design logos for major corporations charge thousands of dollars. The U.S. Air Force recently paid a graphics company $810,000 to change their logo; rumor has it that Jimmy Dean Sausage paid $100,000.

In your area, there are businesses with no logos, some with badly designed logos, or owners who think they can't afford a logo but can if they hire you—and they're all potential customers. If you can come up with something they like—something they can use to identify their businesses, include in their advertising, on signs, on literature, on letterhead, business cards, and so forth— you can earn some money. If they can't afford to pay you in cash, you can trade your designing talents. One computer owner in Washington designed a logo for a restaurant, and they gave him $250 worth of credit. A design he did for a lawn-care service got him six months of free lawn care.

Check the yellow pages, newspapers, and advertising in your area for possible clients. Look at their logos; if you see something that could use some work or redesign, that's a potential client. Just changing a type-style can beef up a logo; if you have a good collection of fonts, you can try that approach. As a beginner, you can design a logo on speculation (it's good practice)—if they like it, you'll get paid; if they don't, you learned something and maybe you can sell that logo later on as your business develops.

There are logo design programs available that contain a variety of basic designs (squares, circles, ovals, wavy lines); you can move them around on the screen, change sizes and colors, and add text. The combinations are almost endless. With a scanner, you can scan an existing logo as a graphic, then manipulate the components into something entirely new using a graphics program. That's what some people do to create logos. To stimulate your logo de-

signing imagination, start by collecting logos from different sources. When you see a nice logo while online, click on it with your right mouse button, choose to save it as a picture, and put it in a file you create called Logos. Over time, you can collect hundreds of logos. They can give you some ideas to apply to designing your clients' logos.

Once the client has a logo, you can offer services that include printing the logo on T-shirts, mugs, mouse pads, caps, and more.

Typesetting Ink has a CD with more than five thousand pieces of clip art and logos that comes with a two-hundred-plus page guide showing the actual contents on paper. Go to their Web site and fill in the form; they'll send you five logo samples at no charge. If you're looking for some unique lettering to go with your logo, there are hundreds of freeware lettering sites online. Click on any of the letters and you'll see samples in different styles that can be downloaded.

LOGO DESIGNING SERVICES:

A New Logo: http://www.allmylogos.com
Company Logo Design: http://www.businesslogo123.com/businesslogo1.htm
Ethernet: http://www.etherdreams.com/services/logo.htm
Level 10 Logo Designing: http://www.leveltendesign.com/design_logos.html
Logo Design AAA: http://www.aaalogo.com/logo_design43.htm

Sample Logo Fonts: http://www.007fonts.com/
Sample Logos: http://www.allmylogos.com/alllinks.htm
Sample Logos: http://www.ibc2001.com/logosamples.html
Sample Logos: http://www.originalwest.com/samples.htm

THE DO-IT-YOURSELF SOLUTION:

TypeSetting Ink: http://www.lotsologos.com/

FREE SOFTWARE:

Free Logo Design: http://www.graphics2000.freeserve.co.uk/

MEDICAL TRANSCRIBER

A medical transcriber sits in front of the computer, listens to audiotapes dictated by health-care professionals, and turns the spoken word into a typed report, usually for a patient's medical file. For every patient who is admitted to the hospital, goes to the emergency room, has an X-ray, or visits a doctor for any reason or for practically any medical incident, reports are generated. The content of the report is usually spoken on tape by the caregiver after the patient leaves. Health-care professionals often outsource the transcribing job, and if you're in the business and offer to pick up the tapes and deliver an error-free report, this might be your kind of home computer business. Ideally, you'll take a course on medical transcribing so you can understand how things are done and how to interpret the medical terms. A transcriber that will accept an assortment of audio tapes is the one piece of equipment that you'll have to purchase. Transcription Service, Career Step, and Global Medical Transcription offer courses, some online.

SOURCES:

CareerStep: http://www.careerstep.com/
Global Medical Transcription: http://medicaltrans.net/
HealthCare Technology: http://www.ehti.net/about.asp

MedPen: http://www.medpen.net/
MedTek: http://www.medtech.net/productsandservices.htm
MedWorld: http://www.medword.com
PCDI: http://www.pcdi.com
Stedman's Dictionary: http://www.stenograph.com/educational/
Ref_StedmanDict.html
SylvanSoft: http://www.sylvansoftware.com/
Transcription Service: http://www.transcriptionservices.net/

MEETING PLANNER

If you live in an area that's a popular vacation spot, you can provide meeting planners around the country with the type of information they need to plan a trouble-free event. You can create a disk called *How to Plan a Trouble-Free Event in [Town Name]* and fill it with the type of information meeting planners need. They want to know about places to hold meetings and accommodations, but they also need the names and phone numbers of caterers, bus and car rental services, lighting specialists, sound system providers, speakers, how to get to and from the airport, and much more. Arrange everything so it can be read and searched with any word processing program.

All this information is readily available for any city in the country from convention and visitors bureaus, tourist associations, and chambers of commerce. You could create a series of How To Plan disks on the major convention and meeting cities, which are (in this order) Las Vegas, Chicago, New York, Los Angeles, Atlanta, New Orleans, Philadelphia, San Francisco, Washington, D.C., and Toronto and Vancouver in Canada. If you know the city personally, you can recommend restaurants, attractions, the best nightspots, and other things to do. You can put your meeting planner series on your Web page and list the cities you cover. You can charge for the disk plus mailing or provide the information via e-mail. I have a database I sell that would be more than three hundred pages long if printed out; I e-mail it to buyers and have never had a problem transmitting it over the Internet despite its size.

To find out what kind of information meeting planners request, call the convention and visitor bureau in some of the major cities and ask, then request copies of their literature and view their Web sites. Some have toll-free numbers. Give them a call to get an idea of what information they can provide. A list of toll-free numbers for states can be found at: http://eventplanner.net/cities/usa/tourist.htm.

MODEM SALES AND INSTALLATION

When a home computer owner discovered there were faster modems than the one she had in her computer, she bought a faster one, hesitantly opened the computer case, and installed it. Over the next few months, friends asked her to help them speed up their Internet connections, so she went into the modem sales and installation business. She found a good, reliable source of modems, made an arrangement to buy them wholesale and sell them retail, and also charged for the installation and configuration.

Many home computer owners are hesitant about opening the case, poking around inside, installing modem cards, connecting a power supply if needed, hooking in the phone line, doing the configuration, assigning ports, and similar tasks. Some modems can now fax directly from a word processing program, but installation takes a little know-how. If you can learn how to do it, there are probably lots of people in your area ready to give you a call. You can charge your clients for your advice, the purchase of the equipment, the trip to their home or office, the installation and configuration, and any instructions they need to make everything work properly.

FAX MODEMS:

BuyMicro: http://www.buymicro.com
Crucial Technology: http://www.computersmarts.com/faxmod.html
ProVantage: http://www.provantage.com/ffmodem_htm

CONNECT MODEMS:

InReach Internet: http://www.56k.com
Modems.Com: http://www.modems.com
National Data Mux: http://www.nationaldatamux.com
PriceScan: http://www.pricescan.com

FREE SOFTWARE:

Fax Phone: http://www.completelyfreesoftware.com/faxphone.zip

MONEY DETECTIVE

It's estimated there are billions of unclaimed dollars out there in dead bank accounts, uncashed checks, safe deposit boxes, unclaimed inheritances, stocks and bonds, money orders, utility deposits, tax returns, uncashed dividends, and so on. I can't think of anyone who wouldn't be interested in knowing if some of that money is theirs. If you can find some for me, I'd be glad to pay you a percentage, and if it's a lot—like $75,000—I'll split it with you (well, maybe).

The only way to find out is to search databases by last names, relatives' names, or any other connection. There are national and individual state databases online. For example, if you and your family are from New York, you can check the New York database to see if there's some money out there somewhere in your name. If there is a record, they inform you how to put in a claim. I found a $50 electric company deposit in New York City dating back to 1955 under my first and last name but couldn't prove I was connected with the party involved, so it's still sitting there.

You can also search by land records in some states to see if there is property involved. Most discoveries involve utility deposits that were made years ago and forgotten, investment returns that were sent to an address then returned because the party no longer lived there, and bank accounts active but long overlooked. The best search site is the National Unclaimed Property Database.

SOURCES:

Find Cash: http://www.findcash.com/
Found Money: http://www.foundmoney.net/main/5049/
money.htm
Missing Money: http://www.missingmoney.com/Main/Index.cfm
New York Database: http://www.osc.state.ny.us/cgibin/db2www/
ouffrm.d2w/input
National Unclaimed Property Database: http://www.nupd.com/
Unclaimed Assets: http://www.unclaimedassets.com/
Unclaimed Money: http://www.unclaimedmoney.com/
Unclaimed Property: http://webinfosearch.com/money/

MUSICIAN'S TIP CARDS

Many solo musicians and musical groups play for a salary as well
as the enjoyment of playing, and if they can earn tips, all the better. A friend of mine played piano in a first-class restaurant and
had a brandy snifter sitting on the piano for tips. On an average
night, he told me, he earned about $25 in tips. I designed him a
request card twice the size of a dollar bill so it could be folded in
half. On the outside, I printed REQUEST and his name at the bottom in small letters. On the inside I printed:

Please Play (first choice) _____ (second
choice) _____ and dedicate it to _____ from
_____. Thank you.

We printed up 250 cards and placed them on the tables in the restaurant. On the first night, he earned more than $70 in tips. The cards were filled out by customers and delivered by the waiters. After two months of use, a card rarely arrived without at least a dollar bill inside, often a $5 bill. Musicians in your area might be interested in this unique approach to improving their tips, so make up a few samples and show them around. Tell them the piano player's story and you're sure to get some orders.

NEWSPAPER PUBLISHER

To become a newspaper publisher, you don't have to publish issues that compete with the *New York Times* or local papers. Your newspaper can be just a few pages of local interest with a large enough distribution to convince local businesses they could profit by paying you for some advertising. Distribution is the key to making money here, so plan on publishing enough copies that the paper is seen around town and earns a reputation for reaching a wide audience. Check with your local print shop for the cost of printing on newsprint paper, which is cheaper than regular bond paper. You can become a reporter yourself or find friends who might be interested in making contributions and getting their writing published. There are syndicates online that provide every-

thing from cartoons to recipes for just pennies; you can use this type of information as a filler. There's a list of syndicates at DOMZ.

SOURCES:

Creators: http://www.creators.com/index2.html
DOMZ: http://dmoz.org/News/Newspapers/Syndicates/

Notepads

With a paper cutter, a clamp, some glue, and notepad binding gauze, you can offer clients personalized notepads ranging in size from 8 ½ by 11 inches down to 4 ½ by 5 ½ inches, which is about half the larger size. Using your word processing or graphics programs, create a design or graphic with the information the clients want on the pad: usually name, address, telephone number, e-mail address, or the like. Choose a type size appropriate for the size of the page. Cut the paper to size, clamp the pages together, apply the glue and gauze, and you have a notepad of twenty-five to fifty sheets.

Contact local businesses and see if they can use notepads for employee use or as a giveaway to their clients. The company name and message along with their logo goes on the bottom; the rest of page is blank.

NUMEROLOGIST

A numerologist is much like an astrologer but uses numbers instead of astrological signs. Numerology is the study of numbers and the occult manner in which they reflect certain aptitudes and character tendencies as an integral part of the cosmic plan. Each letter has a numeric value that provides a related cosmic vibration. The sum of the numbers in someone's birth date and the sum of value derived from the letters in his or her name provide an interrelation of vibrations. Believers feel these numbers show a great deal about character, purpose in life, what motivates, and where talents may lie. Experts in numerology use the numbers to determine the best times for major moves and activities in life.

There are thousands of people who believe in the results of numerological readings—these are your clients. The best way to become a numerologist without any serious training is to use some of the software available. With the software, you'll be able to set up a reading that will include your clients' life path numbers, their expression numbers, their soul urges, birthdays, inner dreams, pinnacles, challenges, gifts, and imitations. Finally, the essence of the year will show what is demanding attention in their lives and where their personal efforts will be focused. When everything is computed, you can provide them with an attractive printout with graphics.

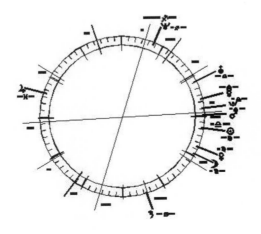

SOURCES:

AspireA1: http://members.aol.com/AspireA1/index8.html
AstrologyK: http://www.astrologyk.com/overview
MU-Online: http://www.muonline.com/english/softwares/
numerology.htm
Numerology: http://www.bonusage.com/English_software/
numerology/Index.html
Numerology: http://www.numeyoga.com/numeyoga/
num_engl.htm
Numerology Now: http://www.numerologynow.com/
Sahara Software: http://www.saharasoftware.com/
Softnumerology.html
Widening Horizons: http://www.wideninghorizons.com/

FREE SOFTWARE:

Decoz: http://www.decoz.com/
Numerology 101: http://www.jumbo.com/hobbies/
files.asp?x_fileid=132401&S=15156&ord=&mV=4
Numerology Calculator: http://www.2near.com/edge

ONLINE STORES

Anyone can put a store on the Internet using software designed
to create online stores or just by creating a Web page. To create an
online store, you first create a Web page, then decide what you
want to include in your offerings. It can be product-specific
(kitchen accessories, clothing) or general (everything you find of
interest). You contact the manufacturers or distributors, see what
kind of arrangement you can make to get paid for your sales efforts, and invite the world to take a look. For clients without a Web
page, your online store can include every item in their inventory
along with photos, specifications, prices, and ordering information. The buyers deal directly with your client. Amazon.com is basically an online store and with a search block, viewers can easily
find the items they're looking for. There are some samples of online stores online at AACart; they offer the software as well.

SOURCES:

A2I: http://www.a2i.com/company.asp
AACart: http://www.aacart.com/index.html
EasyCart: http://www.easycart.com/main.html
ExCara: http://www.excara.com
Hot Spots: http://www.hotscripts.com/detailed/4134.html
TurnAround Computing: http://www.turn.com/catalog2/xlngcat3.htm

ONLINE SUPERMARKET

Online grocery stores on the national level have been having a hard time, but experts say that local online grocery stores that can deliver have a good chance for survival and an opportunity to earn money. The principle is simple: you offer clients a list of items available at whatever grocery store you choose to work with, they send in their shopping lists, and you buy the products and deliver them. Everything except shopping and delivery is done on-

line, so you have to check everyday to see if any customers have sent in lists.

To start, you pick out the grocery store you want to work with. Most people choose a large supermarket like Winn-Dixie, Food World, Publix, or the like. You introduce yourself to the manager so that he or she doesn't wonder why you're walking up and down the aisles on your first visit taking notes. There may be a list of everything available in the store; you can work with that if they'll give you a copy. Otherwise, you can compile a list of everything you want to make available to your clients.

Most lists have more than a hundred items in all categories. It takes a while to set up the service, but eventually you'll have a list of things you can offer clients. Post it on your Web page and you're in business. There's a sample of an online grocery list at My Grocery Checklist. You can use it as a guide to preparing your own list. Over time, you can add items based on clients' needs or delete items that people never order.

You ask your clients to register, and they receive a customer number that they use when they place their orders. They also include their telephone numbers so you can call them if you have any questions. They can choose how to pay: credit card, cash, or check on delivery. You charge your clients a percentage of their purchase or a percentage and a delivery charge. It takes a lot of work but it could prove profitable, because few computer owners are interested in getting involved in a service like this. You might want to hire people to do the shopping and delivery.

SOURCES

BigBear Stores: http://www.bigbearstores.com/
H-E-B Grocery: http://www.hebgrocery.com/
Lowes Foods: http://www.lowesfoods.com/
My Grocery Checklist: http://www.mygrocerychecklist.com
NetGrocer: http://www.netgrocer.com/

Pattern Designing

For clients who like to design their own clothes, you can provide full-sized patterns using design software. The dimensions are entered into the program, and the neckline, sleeve, and other design choices are made by checking the appropriate box. The computer prints out pattern sheets that are taped together to produce full-sized patterns that can be traced onto the fabric. Post a sign in fabric shops around town, explaining what you have to offer.

SOURCES:

Cochenille: http://www.cochenille.com/software.htm
Dress Shop: http://www.livingsoft.com/
Hemmingway: http://www.hemmingaway.com/
sewingsoftware.asp
SewChic: http://www.sewchic.com/software.html
Wild Ginger: http://www.wildginger.com/

PC Doctor

One computer owner in Ohio told me that while he was not a computer expert, he has owned a computer for more than ten years, has dealt with a variety of computer hardware and software problems, and knows quite a bit more about how things work than your average user . . . and average users are his clients. He works out of his home and he's on call twenty-four hours a day if you're willing to pay his fee. One night, a writer called him at 3 A.M. because her word processing program wouldn't save a fifteen-thousand-plus word chapter she'd been working on for seven hours. If she turned off the computer, she would lose the chapter. So she just sat there and looked at it. She felt the $40 was a good investment, so she called him. He told her how to copy the chapter, save it to a disk and also put it somewhere else on the computer, then cross her fingers and reboot. She did (cross her fingers), she did (reboot), and she had copies of the text in her computer, which she copied back into her word processing program and saved everything safely. She also had a backup copy of her writing on disk . . . just in case.

He advises clients over the phone, in person at their offices, by e-mail, and nose-to-nose, depending on the problem and what clients are willing to pay for his services. He can install hardware and software at a client's home or business, or they can bring it to his house, which is the cheapest solution and works well with laptops. He uses a variety of problem detection software programs, some of which are listed below. Some will even boot up computers that are having problems booting up.

At one point last year, he got so many phone calls on software problems that he suggested to some people they get copies of the detection software and try to solve their own problems before they called him. Sometimes it takes hours to run these programs but in the end, the problem is often detected and some how-to-solve-it suggestions are available. It works for more than 50 percent of the people who try it, he says, so it's worth investigating and worth adding to your list of software for sale. There are demo versions of diagnostic software at Europe-Soft USA and Peripheral Test Instruments. There are also companies online that can solve almost any problem if someone locally can't do it. If it's lost data, you can send your client's hard drive to them and they'll attempt to recover it and fix the hard drive if that's the problem.

SOURCES:

BitPipe: http://www.bitpipe.com/data/rlist?t=soft_10_132
DTIData: http://www.dtidata.com
LanEngineering: http://www.lanengineer.com
PCDI: http://www.pcdi.com

SimmTester: http://www.simmtester.com/PAGE/products/doc/docinfo.asp

FREE SOFTWARE:

Euro-Soft USA: http://www.eurosoftusa.com
Peripheral Test Instruments: http://scsitools.com/toolbox.html

PEOPLE FINDER

With any of the people and business locator sites online, you can search for almost anybody in any country. Clients might like to make contact with old friends, schoolmates, business associates, and long-lost military buddies. Each search site is different, but between them all you can search by last name, address, former address, telephone number, Social Security number, military and veterans' organizations, school records, and more. There are reverse searches where you enter a telephone number or address

and they give you the name. Most of the search offerings available on CD are outdated by the time you buy a copy, so stick with the online searches. If you can't find who you're looking for, you can always hire one of the online investigation agencies; they can track down almost anyone.

SOURCES:

AnyWho: http://www.anywho.com/
BigFoot: http://www.bigfoot.com/
BigHugs: http://www.bighugs.com/Find/MilitaryFriends.asp
Military.Com: http://www.military.com
People Search: http://people.yahoo.com/
People Site: http://www.peoplesite.com/
SchoolMates: http://www.schoolmates.com/
U.S. Uncover: http://www.usuncover.com/Main_menu.htm
Who Where: http://www.whowhere.lycos.com/

PHOTO DEVELOPING

You can provide clients with film developing services that provide them with ordinary prints and copies they can post and access

on the Internet. If they can't post them online, you can offer to scan them and create a Web page so everyone they know can take a look. They can also get extra prints, enlargements, high-resolution scans, photo CDs, and slides. Just pick up the client's undeveloped film, print out an order form from PhotoWorks or any of the companies offering this service online, and send it in. They take it from there. During regular processing, the photos are posted online before they arrive by mail; you can provide your clients with the Web site and the user ID so they can see what the photos look like before they arrive. With the photos on your screen, you can right click the best ones and save them in a graphics file.

For clients with photo negatives and slides, you can offer a scanning service that saves the images to disk or CD, preserving the negatives and slides forever. Scanners are available from Hyper-Scan and other companies, including Midwestern Industries in Illinois, which can put as many as two hundred photos on one CD.

SOURCES

Digital Pic: http://www.digitalpicsinc.com/scan_slides.htm
Hyper-Scan: http://www.hyperscan.com/
Midwestern Industries: http://midwestern@film2disk.com
Photo Art Imaging: http://www.photoartimaging.net/
store_to_cd.htm
PhotoWorks: http://www.photoworks.com

POETRY

If you think your poetry writing skills are good enough to impress the general public, you can write a custom poem for a client, print it out in a calligraphy type-style on parchment paper, and frame it as a gift. If clients have poems they've written, you can provide the calligraphy printing service and frame them or get them framed. Gift shops in the area might be interested in offering your poem writing services to their clients. Create a small promotional card or business card in the calligraphy style and ask

them to post it on their countertops or walls. You can also create a framed sample. They offer your services and get a commission on each sale. Calligraphy type-styles can be found in the Font section.

PRESS RELEASE MAILINGS

Businesses spend hundreds of millions of dollars a year on advertising. Most get their message out to the public by purchasing ad space in publications and sending out press releases. If they can get one promotional piece published in a national newspaper or magazine, they get free exposure . . . and press releases are published at no charge. Magazines and newspapers publish press releases so they can inform their readers of new products and services. When a major car company introduces a new feature, for example, you can bet the auto magazines will mention it free so their readers can get the news. Auto magazines compete with each other over who can get the news out the fastest, so an interesting news release can get published fast.

Would a local restaurant be interested in announcing the arrival of their new chef and her specialties? Would a local hospital want to announce the arrival of new equipment that makes a procedure safer, faster, and less complicated? They would, and getting exposure in a local newspaper or magazine is a promotional coup.

When a local business in Florida introduced a new type of boat trailer, a home computer owner sent a press release to all the newspapers in the state, consumer magazines (magazines read by the general public), and boating trade magazines (magazines read by owners and managers of boating stores) via e-mail. She attached a photo as a .jpeg file the editors could download. Several of the publications mentioned the trailer and showed the photo—and this exposure resulted in additional sales for the trailer company. The cost to the trailer company? Just what they paid the computer owner to collect the publication names, write the release, and e-mail it to the editors.

You can check around your area for clients looking for exposure of some sort, or write to potential clients you discover on the Internet or read about in magazines. You can send them an email asking if they'd be interested in you sending a press release to hundreds or thousands of newspapers and magazines around the world, around the country, around the state—their choice based on what they want to pay. Your clients can range from businesses to political candidates who don't have their own public relations firm.

Of course, you need the email addresses of these publications, and there are several ways you can get them. You can search online by subject (accounting, art, books, decorating) and over time compile a good list. There are databases available that provide this information. My EMail Publisher and World Newspapers 2002–2003 lists the email addresses or Web sites of more than ten thousand newspapers (by country and U.S. states), magazines (by subject), and book publishers (alphabetically). You can search the list using any word processing program. If you want to send a press release to women's magazines, Canadian newspapers, or college publications, this is one place to find the addresses. Once you have your list, you can insert the press release into your email, enter the addresses, and reach hundreds of editors with one click of your mouse.

If clients would rather do it themselves, you can provide them with the addresses on a disk. They can load the disk, enter the addresses in their email, and do their own mailing. Providing clients with a database like this can be a profitable computer-related business.

SOURCES:

Crown Industries: http://www.bulkemailit.cjb.net
EMail Publisher 2002-2003: http://philcox.homestead.com/email.html
ExtractorPro: http://www.extractorpro.com

PRIVATE DETECTIVE AGENCY

If someone is hiring an employee through a classified ad, planning on getting married, or signing a contract with a total stranger, they might be interested in knowing a little more—or a lot more—about that person's background. This who-are-they? information applies to almost everybody they don't know but plan on letting into their lives, including baby-sitters, tenants, business associates, and more.

There are ways to do basic investigating over the computer by contacting city and state records, but like most complex projects, this type of computer business is best left to the experts. There are records online that are open to the public, including land records; court records of judgments, liens, bankruptcies, and lawsuits; licensing records; driver's license information; and more, but checking out the online links to fifty states is a tedious job and will probably turn up little if any information. In some states, like Florida, you can access online sex offender records and, for a fee, driver's license information, but that's about it. In other states, most records are not easily accessible.

For local investigations, call your local courthouse and find out what records are open to the public. If someone you're investigat-

ing lives in the area and has a criminal record or was sued, you might be able to find out. The best solution is to use your computer to communicate with online investigators. They're all over the place on the Internet, so you can contact some and see what they offer, how much they charge, and how they conduct an investigation. When you find someone you think you can work with, you can start your investigation business. You can suggest to clients that they put together some kind of form a potential employee or someone they plan on doing business with can fill out. The information should include name (maiden name if married), date of birth, current and past addresses, Social Security number, former employers (at least two or three previous jobs), driver's license number, and references. Include a paragraph that authorizes you or your agent to conduct a credit search. This is the type of information most investigators need to get started.

Most basic checks cost around $30 or so, and you can add something for your part in the investigation. More detailed checks cost more. Most people in your area don't have any idea how to conduct an investigation, so contact apartment and home rental agencies, businesses, and other potential clients, tell them about your computerized detective agency, and you'll probably get some takers.

SOURCES:

Dun and Bradstreet: http://www.dnb.com
Free Edgar: http://www.freedgar.com
Hoover's Online: http://www.hooversonline.com
How To Investigate: http://howtoinvestigate.com
PCDI: http://www.pcdi.com

REAL ESTATE ONLINE

More and more real estate agents are going online and offering their services to clients around the world. But not every real estate agent has the capacity (or the desire) to create a Web page, pay whatever it costs, and start listing properties. Surprisingly, there are real estate agents out there who aren't even aware of the benefits of being online. An online Realtor can reach a wide audience and show them what's available in their area. They can create different Web pages for different sections of town, show interior and

exterior photos of properties, as well as detailed descriptions, information on schools, taxes, and more. This increases the likelihood that someone relocating will take a look, find something interesting, and give them a call.

You can provide these services to real estate offices in your area in several different ways. You can design and sell them a Web site of their own, offer them the chance to share a Web site with other agencies or businesses in the area, or let them post their listings on your Web pages. One computer owner in Boston has enough Web site space to create twenty or thirty Web pages, so he uses his allotment to create a page for each of his clients. One client lists properties within a fifty-mile radius of the city; another covers only the downtown area.

Your clients will probably be small real estate offices and Realtors who don't have the resources or time to display their offerings online. With your search engine, check for Web sites of local Realtors, then compare them with the Realtors listed in the yellow pages of your phone book. Those not online are your potential clients, so call or send them a flyer or sales letter and see if you can get some response. If they don't want their own page or their own Web site account, you can rent them a full page, half page, or quarter page. Any photos they provide can be scanned and posted along with property descriptions.

RECIPE SERVICE:

Got a client or friend looking for the recipe for some exotic dish, Mexican or French food, or just another way to prepare ground beef? You can supply a list of options along with information on calories, fat content, cooking advice, and variations few people would even consider. There are hundreds of recipes at Meal Master; a search online will reveal thousands of recipes, including those popular in foreign countries. Contact some local restaurants and offer them the opportunity to start offering their customers something different, then do a recipe search based on their criteria and send them a multipage recipe report.

SOURCES:

CookenPro: http://www.cooken.com/
Meal Master: http://www.mealmaster.com/
Mindspring: http://www.mindspring.com/~cathylielausis/
rprograms.htm
Now You're Cooking: http://www.ffts.com/

FREE SOFTWARE:

AZZCardFile: http://www.azzcardfile.com/recipe/
recipe_software.html
CookWare: http://www.cookn.com/
Regi Dean's Recipes: http://www.homeplansoftware.com/
recipe.htm

RESELLING ONLINE

A reseller purchases a service or product from a provider, then resells these services or products to others via computer for a profit. In some cases, the profit is 10 to 15 percent of the sale, but

it could be up to 50 percent. If you're reselling a computer program that sells for $50, you can earn $5 or more for each sale and
all you have to do is act as the go-between for the buyer and the
seller.

Some online companies will make you an affiliate member if
you place a hyperlink on your Web page that viewers can click on.
They're automatically sent to the host Web site; you are paid for
each lead and sale that originates from your page. Another option
is to set up a separate Web site that promotes the host's services or
products; you forward all leads to the host so you can keep track of
your contributions. For each sale, a commission or flat payment is
made. The reselling involves investigation services like Tenant-
Check, domain names and online services, books and other products, and almost anything you can think of. In fact, you can
approach anyone with something to sell on- or offline and offer to
act as a reseller for a commission or flat fee.

If you're a romance book lover, for example, you can contact
publishers of romance books and offer to post information about
their books on your Romance Reader's Web page. Every time
someone buys a book through your Web site, you earn a commis-

sion. One book publisher told me, "I pay bookstores 40 percent or more to sell my books; why not pay a computer owner who's helping me sell books the same?"

A computer owner in Georgia found more than a dozen business-related software programs and put them on her Business Software Web page. She shows a copy of the product package (downloaded from the manufacturer's Web page with permission) and a brief description and the price. The readers of the page order through her; she forwards the order via e-mail to the sales department and earns a commission on each sale. The procedures for ordering vary with each company and should be clarified in advance. It's best to have a contact person at the other end who will process your orders. There are far too many reselling opportunities to list here, so you can start by searching with Copernic, Google, or other search engines under the word *reseller* and see what comes up. You can also approach a company via their Web page and offer to act as a reseller. Work only with reputable companies.

SOURCES:

20-20 Software: http://www.2020software.com/associates.htm
Cabinet Internet: http://www.thk.net/uk/jm/
Highlights For Children: http://www.highlightsaffiliates.com/index.html
Linux WebHost: http://www.linuxwebhost.com/resellerplans.html
MongoSoft: http://www.mango.com/partners/
TenantCheck: http://www.tenantchk.com/Resellers.htm

Resumé Writer

Anyone looking for work could use the help of someone who knows how to put a good resumé together. There are software programs that guide you through the most popular formats, so all you need from clients is the information to fill out the form; then you print it out and collect your payment. Chances are good they'll get

better results with a resumé created by this professional software than one they create themselves. Many of the programs explain why information should and should not be included; you can share this with your client.

SOURCES:

DamnGood Resumes: http://www.damngood.com/ready/
Emotional Desktop: http://www.emotional.com/wallpaper.htm
Resume Blowout: http://www.resumeblowout.com/
WebResume: http://www.webresume.org/
Whirlwind Software: http://www.wwtech.com/trr.htm

FREE SOFTWARE:

QuickStart: http://www.collegegrad.com/jobsearch/69.shtml
Resume Pro: http://www.freesohojobs.com/deals.html

SCREEN SAVERS

Using any of the screen saver programs, you can create a group of photos, documents, or graphics that can be provided to clients on a disk they can present to their customers. One computer owner in Michigan creates disks with ten or fifteen images that flash on the screen when the computer is idle in the screen saver mode. His clients are families that have him create screen saver disks as gifts. Businesses might be interested in presenting their customers with a free screen saver that flashes their products or photos of their services on screen along with their name and telephone number. A photographer can use screen savers to show potential clients samples of his or her work.

SOURCES:

Make Your Own Screensaver: http://www.customsavers.com/
Screen Saver Studio: http://www.screensaverstudio.com/
Stardust Screensaver: http://www.stardustsoftware.com/sstoolkit/

FREE SOFTWARE:

Acez: http://www.acez.com
Screen Gizmos: http://www.screengizmos.com/

SECRETARIAL SERVICES

The U.S. Department of Labor predicts that in the next six years, there will be openings for as many as nine hundred thousand secretarial positions and 25 percent or more will be offsite, which means they will be working somewhere other than their employer's office. With the right clients, you can earn a comfortable income as an off-site secretary or data entry person, doing exactly what you would do in an office without leaving your home and in or out of your pajamas (your choice). The skills required range from simple typing to entering data in databases, maintaining files, editing, and general office skills. The advantages for a business hiring a secretary or computer operator offsite are many: they don't have to supply a computer or workspace, don't have to offer health and vacation benefits (if you work as an outside contractor), and can offer lower salaries than those for office workers. All of this is negotiable and should be discussed in detail before

you accept any position. You can search any of the job databases online as well as the classified section of your newspaper.

SENIOR CHECK-IN SERVICES

Programs like ElderCheck by DemoSource can automatically call clients' phone numbers several times a day to see if they're okay, reminding them of schedules, when to take medication, and other important needs. If clients fail to respond to the call, this could mean they need help, especially if they're seniors living alone with medical problems. You can call members of their families, neighbors, or emergency medical services, depending on what previous arrangements have been made.

The programs allow you to enter the numbers to call, the times to call, and help numbers in case of an emergency. The computer dials the number through your modem; if there is no answer, it dials the backup help number. This service can also be provided to parents for checking on their children when they're away from home. In addition to the elderly, clients could be nursing homes, health-care providers, hospitals, physicians monitoring their patients at home, and church groups.

There are several services and programs that provide monitoring of the elderly or others who might require it.

SOURCES:

Fidelity Alarm: http://www.fidelitytelealarm.com/
Lifeline Systems: http://www.lifelinesys.com/
Senior Technologies: http://www.seniortechnologies.com/
TeleAlarm: http://www.fidelitytelealarm.com/
UK Software: http://www.uksoftware.com/

SIGNATURE SCANNING

There are services that will take a signature sample from clients and convert it into a font version that they can use to sign letters and documents they create with their word processing programs.

The fonts are supplied on disk and can be loaded into a word processing program. This eliminates the need for clients to hand-sign each document and letter. They position the cursor at the end of the document, click on the font, and the signature appears. An executive's assistant can use the font to sign the executive's signature; a password can be inserted to eliminate any chance of someone using the font without permission. Actually, you can scan any signature and save it as a graphic that can be inserted in a document. Because graphics can be sized (made larger or smaller), they can fit anywhere on a document and be adjusted to size.

SOURCES:

Digital Media Centre: http://www.mun.ca/cc/dmc/signature.shtml
Parish Data Systems: http://www.parishdatainc.com/bitmap.htm
Signature Software: http://www.vletter.com/website/default.html

SPECIAL OFFER CARDS

An auto shop might want to offer clients a free oil filter with an oil change or a tire rotation with a tune-up. A restaurant can offer

two-for-one nights, or a bookstore might give a $5 credit with the purchase of $50 worth of books over a period of time.

You can provide these types of cards and the ideas by approaching businesses and explaining the benefits of making special offers. The cards can be designed with your word processing or graphics program, cut to size, and presented to clients for distribution to their customers. You can use business card stock if the client doesn't object to the size.

SYNDICATED COLUMNIST

Got an idea for a newspaper or magazine column, something that can appear regularly in local or national publications? Publications are looking for people like you who can provide readers with information on everything from gardening to relationships. Syndicated columnists have their columns published in numerous publications and earn a few dollars here and a few dollars there. Those few dollars can really add up. Because there's no overlap in readership (people in Texas don't read newspapers published in Florida), a Texas editor would have no objection to buying your

column if it's already appearing in Florida and other state newspapers. You can put together some samples, check the newspaper databases online, e-mail one or two, and see what happens.

SOURCES:

E-Mail Publisher/World Newspapers: http://philcox.homestead.com/email.html
Gebbie Press: http://www.gebbieinc.com/

TECHNICAL CONSULTANT

A few months ago, I'd have gladly paid someone to answer two questions I had about using a software program that came with my computer and how I could set up my Outlook Express mailbox. The instructions that came with the software were difficult to understand, and tech support never answered my e-mail requests for help. If you were an online consultant, you could have earned your first Internet dollars from me.

Computer owners are always running into problems and while

technical help is available, it often includes long waits on the telephone or, worse, no answer at all. You e-mail tech support, and often they tell you they'll get back to you within forty-eight to seventy-two hours. I don't know about you, but I can't wait two to three days to get an answer. I want answers fast, and I'll be glad to pay for them. One computer user in California does just that. He's online almost twenty-four hours a day, and if you have a question, you can e-mail or instant message him. If you have a credit card, he'll give you the answer within minutes. On the four occasions I've used him, he's given me the correct answer three times. If he can't help, there's no charge. If you have this kind of computer know-how, you could become a consultant. In most cases, you listen to the client's problem, then access the software manufacturer's Web page and search for solutions. If you find something, you can provide the client with an answer and get paid.

TONER CARTRIDGE REMANUFACTURING

Everybody with a printer or fax machine deals with the toner cartridge replacement process. Buying them new ranges from $25 for a small cartridge to up to $150 for laser jet printer cartridge. You can buy the supplies needed to refill any cartridges with toner and start a local business. Contact business offices around town, explain your refilling services, and offer to pick up and deliver if necessary. The refill process is fairly simple; all the how-to information comes with the supplies you'll be ordering. If you don't want to get your hands dirty, you can buy remanufactured cartridges for every type of copier, printer, and fax machine and act as the middle-person between your client and the cartridge suppliers.

SOURCES:

Clarity Imaging: http://www.clarityimaging.com/
laser_toner_cartridges_d.html
MAPPS: http://mappsonline.com/
PCDI: http://www.pcdi.com
Spectrum West: http://www.spectrumwest.com/
Supplies USA: http://www.suppliesusa.com/

UPS Sales

UPS, in addition to being the initials of United Parcel Service, also means "uninterrupted power supply." Clients can buy their units from you and pay you to come to their offices or homes and install them. Installation is simple: you plug the computer into the UPS and plug the UPS into the wall . . . that's it. The UPS stores enough power to keep a computer on long enough for the user to save what they were working on in case of a power failure. The amount of time that power is supplied varies with the unit. The more you pay, the longer it provides power. In rural areas, where heavy snowfall can down power lines, UPS units are very popular. Other computer users say they're in demand in large cities where power failures are frequent.

SOURCES:

CellPower: http://www.cellpower.com.tw/
Jetta Tech: http://www.jettatech.com
Machine Runner: http://www.machinerunner.com
Optimum Power: http://www.optimumpower.com/ups.htm
PC Upgraders: http://www.pcupgraders.com

Used-Car Database

Take a look at the classified ads in the newspapers in your area and surrounding areas. Chances are you'll find hundreds of used cars for sale, so there's certainly a market for a convenient way for computer users to see what used cars are available in their area. Create a Web page that lists cars by make and model, following the format of the classified ad section of the newspaper, but with the addition of photos. Contact used-car dealers and invite them to list their offerings. You can charge them for each listing or work on a pay-per-sale basis. For every car they sell through your Web page, they pay you, say, $10. You can put a link on your Web page that will take the viewer to a database of used cars. The database can be created using a program that sorts entries by year, price, make, and model, or it could be simply a list of cars by make cre-

ated with your word processing program. Clients looking for a particular car, regardless of its location, can pay you to search the Internet and see if you can find one somewhere in the country.

SOURCES:

Cardbox: http://www.cardbox.co.uk/
RecordKeeper: http://www.recordkeeper.com/

VIDEO CONFERENCING

Talking over the computer through a mike and speakers is one thing, but having the actual image of the person you're talking to on the screen is the ultimate communication tool. Video conferencing is being used by many major corporations, but the technology has developed to the point where it's affordable for even small businesses and individuals. There are people in your area who might like to set up a video conferencing system with business associations, friends, and family members. Both sides need the software, a video camera, speaker, mike, and a means of connection—a telephone or an Internet connection.

All these components are available in a package that is easily installed and costs, in some cases, a few hundred dollars. Try hooking up a system with your own computer and that of a family member or friend; once you're up and running, you can offer this service locally. Dwyco offers a free copy of the software you will need that you can use with an inexpensive video camera (less than $100 at any computer store) and your present computer speakers and microphone.

SOURCES:

Computer Geeks: http://www.compgeeks.com/
products.asp?cat=VID
Desktop Video Products: http://www3.ncsu.edu/dox/video/
products.html
First Virtual Communications: http://www.cuseeme.com/
Hardware For Video Conferencing: http://www.cs.columbia.edu/
~hgs/rtp/hardware.html

FREE SOFTWARE:

Dwyco: http://www.dwyco.com/

WEB PAGE DESIGNER

You can offer individuals and businesses in the area a Web page design service at a price no one else in the area can beat if you stick to simple page designs and use services that provide page templates. You can create and post the page online all in one day. Then, clients can give their URL (the Web site address) to friends, customers, and so on.

One of the easiest Web page creation sources is Homestead, which doesn't require any experience other than a good eye for page layout. You start with a preset design, choosing from several options with color blocks and layouts, or a blank white page. Click on T and you enter text. Click on the graphic icon and you enter graphics. Click on the blocks and you can move things around on the page until they're to your client's liking. There are lots of graphics and images to choose from and an assortment of type-

styles. Up until recently, Homestead was free; they've started charging for their services now, though, so you'll have to decide if it's worth your investment. I have about twenty Web pages on Homestead, including my personal page at http://philcox.home stead.com/writers.html.

You can offer clients a Web page forever, twelve months, six months, three months—whatever they're willing to pay for. If you design a page and three months later they stop paying, you can change the Web site address so no one will be able to access it except you. If they decide later to pay again, you can change the name back to the original.

One client of a computer user in Florida is a photographer. Her page has a photo of herself, some text explaining what she does, some sample photos, and an e-mail link. Another client sells her own books, and people accessing the Web site can order with a credit card by clicking on one of the credit card links.

If you're considering this as a business, you can offer clients two choices. They can sign on with Homestead under their name, pay the fee, give you their password, and you design the page for them. The more profitable option, however, is for you to sign on, pay the fee, then sell the space to them. There are several free Web page services online, including AOL, so shop around until you find something you like and that's easy to use. Most big-time Web page services require that you know something about HTML, the Web page design language, which can be very difficult to use.

SOURCES:

American Online: http:aol.com
CoffeeCup Software: http://www.coffeecup.com/
Homestead: http://homestead.com
PCDI: http://www.pcdi.com
Trellix: http://www.trellix.com/
Web Developer: http://www.webdeveloper.com/

FREE SOFTWARE:

BellsnWhistles: http://www.bellsnwhistles.com/
Free Web Templates: http://www.elated.com/
Reptile: http://www.sausage.com/reptile/

WEDDING INVITATION PRINTING

Using any of the calligraphy fonts available and card stock designed for invitations, you can provide clients with wedding and other invitations at half the cost of professionally prepared invitations. Some professional invitations are engraved, and the cost is very high. You can't produce engraved invitations, but by using the best card stock you can get from any of the paper sources listed elsewhere in the book and a good calligraphy font, you can produce invitations that are almost as good as the high-priced options. There are some samples and free downloads at the Web sites below. Complete invitation software kits are available from Wedding Invitations.

SOURCES:

Elfring Fonts: http://64.21.138.30/script.htm
Rosemary Hall Calligraphy: http://calligraphyfonts.com/

Script and Calligraphy Fonts: http://www.downlinx.com/
proghtml/127/12726.htm
The Scriptorium: http://www.fontcraft.com/scriptorium/
Wedding Invitations: http://members.gotnet.net/eperillo/
Wedding/Invitation.htm

WHO'S WHO DIRECTORY

Become the editor of a local Who's Who directory, the ultimate
Who's Who publication in your area. Using your world processing
program, you can produce a book listing people in your area who
want to be recognized for their achievements. Being listed in a
Who's Who directory is looked at as a prestige achievement and
an honor, even if people pay to be listed, which isn't unusual.
There are regional Who's Who directories (*Who's Who in the
American Southeast,* for example) that charge for each entry and
offer those listed a discount on buying copies once it's published.
People buy their stars on the Walk of Fame in California and
movie studios pay for advertising so their actors and actresses can
win awards, so people are not always judged on their merits.

For a one-time fee, with different rates for different page space (quarter or half page), your clients supply the information and a photo, and you publish the directory. If you're not familiar with the format for directories, check out *Who's Who in America* at your library or at their Web site. A sample listing of Hillary Rodham Clinton is below.

You can put an application on a Web page, have people interested in being listed in your directory fill it in, and e-mail or regular mail it with their application fee. All of this is confidential; no one needs to know the person listed paid a fee to be recognized. Upon publication, each person listed gets a free copy and can buy additional copies at a discount. Who's Who directories aren't cheap because they have to be great-looking hardcover books. Check with printers in your town about the cost of publishing the book. You can charge as much as $50 a copy regardless of how much you pay to have it published.

You can test the market in advance by announcing your plan to publish a directory; anyone interested can go to your Web page for information. You can also place ads in newspapers and call, snail mail, or e-mail potential clients, especially those who have recently been in the news, those who own local businesses, or people active in local activities and charities. Set up a mock-up of your cover and post it on your Web page. Make it look as close to *Who's Who in America* as possible. As a regional directory, it can open with an introduction explaining the contributions to the community made by the people listed, giving a history of your town and the progress it's made over the year, and including some old town photos; then the biographical entries are listed alphabetically by last name.

You can also create an online directory, similar to that at http://www.hitl.washington.edu/projects/knowledge_base/who. html. Check one of the listings and you'll see a biography, photograph, and e-mail link if they have one. If you have Web page access, you can put something like this online for almost nothing and eliminate the hard copy, reducing the cost of being listed to something more reasonable.

Clinton, Hillary Rodham (1947–)

Democratic member of the United States Senate from New York (2001–) and wife of United States president Bill Clinton (1993–2001). During her husband's presidency, she became a powerful symbol of the changing role and status of women in American society. Her election to the U.S. Senate while being first lady was unprecedented in U.S. history. Born in Chicago, Illinois, Hillary Rodham was the first student ever asked to give the commencement address at Wellesley College, where she earned her bachelor's degree in 1969. At Yale Law School, she met her future husband, Bill Clinton, and her lifelong mentor, Marian Wright Edelman; Edelman founded the Children's Defense Fund, an organization that lobbies for children's welfare. Rodham worked there as a staff attorney for a year after graduating from law school in 1973 and later chaired the organization's board. In 1974, after working for the special U.S. House panel investigating a possible impeachment of President Richard Nixon, she moved to Arkansas, where she began teaching law at the University of Arkansas. She and Bill Clinton were married a year later. A daughter, Chelsea, was born in 1980.

SOURCES:

Who's Who in America: http://www.marquiswhoswho.com

WILL MAKER

Surprisingly, you don't have to be a lawyer to prepare your own will or advise a client on how to make out a simple will. Finances permitting, advising a client to get a lawyer involved is best; you shouldn't really get involved in providing legal assistance to clients. Still, a simple will that doesn't involve a lot of property and assets can be just that . . . simple. In fact, most states will recognize a handwritten will if it's legible and signed by a couple of witnesses, but following the actual will format is best. There are will software programs that will guide you through the process step by step. You interview your clients, fill in the blanks, and present them with a valid will. They can have it witnessed, sign it, and store it in a safe place.

SOURCES:

Blue Sky Distributors: http://www.blueskyd.com
Family Will Kit: http://www.livingtrusts.net/willkit.html
Nolo Law For All: http://www.nolo.com/product/
Will Software: http://www.gamblingsystems.com/legal-kits/ will-kit.html

Word Processing and Typing Tutor

With few exceptions, if you can't type and are looking for a job, chances are you'll be passed up in favor of people who can not only type but are familiar with the major word processing programs—MSWord and WordPerfect. Many job hunters, then, need some help in learning how these programs work and how to use a keyboard; you can set up training classes for individuals or small groups. There are typing programs that automate the entire process along with the tests the clients can take to determine their progress.

SOURCES:

Advanced Speed Typing: http://www.programfiles.com/index.asp?ID=17130
Animated Beginner's Typing: http://www.programfiles.com/index.asp?ID=446
Mavis Beacon: http://www.mavisbeacon.com/Default.htm
TouchTyping Tutor: http://www.typingmaster.com/
TuxTyping: http://www.geekcomix.com/dm/tuxtype/

MONEYMAKING SCAMS

If you're interested in earning money with your home computer, working only a few hours a day, there are business offers online that guarantee you can make $2,000 to $5,000 a week if you send $29.95 to their post office box in Brooklyn, New York. Sounds like a great deal . . . but I'm curious. If they can tell you how to make $2,000 to $5,000 a week, why don't they hire fifty people at, say, double the minimum wage, tell them what to do, and let them start earning that kind of money, turning it over to the employers. They could earn fifty times that $2,000 to $5,000 every week!

Scams like this feed off our need to believe that there has to be an easier way to make money than how we're doing it now. If they make the right pitch, they figure they can get rich with your $29.95 and the thousands of other $29.95s. Some scams just promise a few extra dollars; others promise riches for everything from stuffing envelopes to owning your very own shopping mall Web site. In a way, it's easier to be sucked into the smaller scam requiring only $5 or $10, because most people feel they have less to lose if it doesn't work out and much to gain from such a small investment if it does.

Scams involve a clever use of psychology. When you see something promoting some unbelievable home business or computer opportunity along with photos of sunset beaches and computer owners living in high-rise apartments with luxury cars parked in a nearby underground garage, you wonder . . . *Can I do this too?* Probably not. It's a cliché, but it's like they say: "If it sounds too good to be true, it probably is."

The two things these scams have in common is the low fee you have to pay to get in on the deal and the fact that you're not going to earn anywhere near the money they promise. They might offer a money-back guarantee, but that's usually an unenforceable promise. Once you send them the money, it's probably gone forever.

Internet scams are no different than non-Internet scams. They make promises, ask you to send them money, and the road to riches lies ahead. The only problem is, when you get there, it's a dead end. I get moneymaking offers via e-mail all the time; I've have had as many as forty in one day. If you go looking for moneymaking opportunities on the Internet on your own, you'll probably get similar promises and similar disappointments.

Here are just a few samples:

- The government is interested in boosting the economy and wants people to start businesses online. To assist, they offer grants and funding. Who's giving the money away, how much is available, what type of online businesses they're financing, and how to apply for the money is all in the $15 book they offer to send you. The book is actually a booklet of about thirty-six pages, and it's an exact duplicate of a government publication available free from the Consumer Information Center in Pueblo, Colorado. It covers government grants in general, usually for small non-Internet businesses and for educational purposes. Of little use to people like you and me.
- A company wants you to send e-mail for major corporations from your home computer. For $25, they'll supply you with a list of corporations that are looking for people like you who can spend a few hours a day at the computer. They tell you these companies usually spend tens of thousands of dollars on postage and have decided it's cheaper to pay you 25 cents for each e-mail message you send than paying the post office first-class postage. For the $26 plus $4.95 for postage, you get a list of company names and addresses taken from some business directory you can view on the Internet free of charge. You're supposed to contact the company and offer your e-mail services. All of these companies have sophisticated computer equipment that can do their own bulk e-mailing for pennies per hundred, so they're not interested in paying you 25 cents per mailing.

- You get an e-mail from some folks in a Third World country. They have hundreds of thousands or millions of dollars they want to transfer to an American bank account but can't because of regulations in their country. They need someone like you to help; they will pay you 20 percent of the transferred funds. They want a copy of your driver's license, your bank account number, the name and address of your bank, and other information. Since they don't know you, they ask you to send $50 as good-faith money through a bank transfer. Then they'll provide you with the name of their bank and tell you how to start the transaction.

- I got an e-mail from a company that said they would put my Web site addresses at the top of all the major search engines on the Internet for $10 each. If someone does a search for anything I offer, my Web page would come out on the top of the list. Impossible.

- Some folks ask you to put a banner ad or link on your Web pages that will allow viewers to click and go directly to their Web page. They sell everything from herbal medicines to books; for every sale that results from your link, you get a commission. This doesn't cost you any money, but you're providing them with free advertising and never get any commissions.

- Some people e-mail you and invite you to join an elite group of computer moneymakers. All the free information is available at their Web site, which they list in big letters. You click on the link and the Web page comes up. Right there in the middle is the free report icon. You click on it. To gain access, you have to be a member, fill out an application, and send some money with your credit card. When they get payment, they give you the password. When you get there, there isn't any usable information.

- Do you have any money in state or federal banks, money that belonged to relatives who have died? They'll send you a report for $25, listing all the people with your last name in a particular state who have money in dead accounts. If you can prove you're related, they tell you the money is yours. There are sites online that will provide this information free—it's one of the projects in this book.

- The ad or e-mail says that if you're interested in learning how to make money over the Internet, call (900) 555-1234. The call costs $1.50 a minute, and they'll keep you on the line for as long as they can. When a voice comes online, it's a tape offering to sell you some type of moneymaking book or report.

- A company is looking for customers in your area, so they e-mail you and offer you $1 for every name, address, and phone number you can copy from the phone book and e-mail them. If this were a valid offer, you could scan an entire directory page with your flatbed scanner (there must be at least 100 to 150 entries on each page), send them the list, and earn $100 to $150 per mailing. Nobody is going to pay that kind of money when names, addresses, and phone numbers are available through search engines online.

- Via e-mail, some folks offer you a special report for $10 that lists five of the best moneymaking ideas on the Internet. If you don't earn ten times that much in the first two weeks, they'll return your money and give you a free gift. The report is of no value, has no good ideas, the free gift is a ballpoint pen, and if you ask for your money back, they just ignore you.

- You're invited to add your name and address to the bottom of a mailing list, send $5 to the person listed at the top of the list, and e-mail it to friends. Then sit back and wait. This is a online chain letter and illegal in the United States. Of course, no one ever gets any money.

- Multilevel marketing involves you sending money for a product, then selling the product over the Internet; for every sale, you get a commission. You ask other computer owners you know to do the same and eventually, the pyramid pays you for every sale.

- There's a guy in California who operates an online auction similar to the one on eBay. All the items listed are priced low. The catch is, they're also fictitious. If you make a bid and win, you send your money and get nothing in return. E-mail him about the problem and the mail comes back undeliverable.

- A company in Georgia will advertise your Web pages free in twenty-three computer newsletters and magazines if you buy a subscription to ten or more. They provide a list of major magazines and the subscription rates. You fill in an application, give them your credit card number, and start receiving the publications . . . but never see your Web page mentioned. When you write the magazine, they say you have to deal with the subscription agent who sold you the subscription. When you try his e-mail and mailing address, they are no longer valid.

The National Fraud Information Center (NFIC) will answer questions about online scams and provide information on how and where to report frauds. Their e-mail address is nfic@internetmci.com; the Web site is located at http://www.fraud.org.

RESOURCES

COMPUTER MAGAZINES

Computer magazines are a great source of information and moneymaking ideas. In each issue, you'll find articles on projects that might work in your area, reviews of new software, and advertisements that could be a good source of the stuff you need to run your business. All the publication Web site addresses listed were current as of press time, but time marches on; what's here today might not be here tomorrow. If you run into a dead end, you can search for the publication by its name or go to Yahoo.com and search for *computer magazines*.

Advisor Magazine: http://www.advisor.com/
Australian Personal Computer: http://apcmag.com/
BlueButtBunny: http://www.bluebuttbunny.com/
Boardwatch Magazine: http://boardwatch.internet.com/
Cadalyst: http://www.cadonline.com/
Chip Online: http://www.chip-online.com/
CIO: http://www.cio.com/
c/Net: http://www.cnet.com/
Computer Bits: http://www.computerbits.com/
Computer Business Review: http://www.cbronline.com/
Computer Currents Interactive: http://www.currents.net/
Computer Dealer News: http://www.plesman.com/cdn/
index.html
Computer Edge Online: http://www.computeredge.com/
Computer Gaming World: http://www.computergaming.com/
Computer News Daily: http://computernewsdaily.com/
Computer Paper: http://www.tcp.ca/
Computer Post: http://www.cpost.mb.ca/
Computer Retail Week: http://www.crw.com

Computer World: http://www.computerworld.com/
CyberStuff: http://www.cyberstuff.net/what_is_cyberstuff.htm
eWeek: http://www.zdnet.com/eweek/
Gadget: http://www.gadgetnews.com/
Game Revolution: http://www.game-revolution.com/
Inside Games: http://www.insidegames.com
Intelligamer: http://www.intelligamer.com/
JAVA Pro: http://www.java-pro.com/
JAVA World: http://www.javaworld.com/
Juiced GS: http://www.wbwip.com/juiced.gs/
Mac Addict: http://www.macaddict.com/
Mac Central: http://www.maccentral.com/
Maximum PC: http://www.maximumpc.com/
MD Computing: http://www.mdcomputing.com
Net Guide: http://www.netguide.com/
Network Computing: http://www.networkcomputing.com/
New Media Review: http://www.nmreview.com/
Next Generation: http://www.next-generation.com/
On Magazine: http://www.onmagazine.com/
PC Zone: http://www.pczone.co.uk
Reviewboard Magazine: http://www.reviewboard.com/
Start Computing: http://www.smartcomputing.com/
Ugeek Magazine: http://www.ugeek.com

FREE COMPUTER MAGAZINES

You can get a free subscription to the magazines listed below by filling in a subscription form at their Web sites.

Application Development Trends: http://www.adtmag.com/
qualcard.htm
CIO: http://www.cio.com/
Component Strategies: http://www.sigs.com/cso/qualform/
DB2 Magazine: http://www.db2mag.com/
DBMS: http://www.dbmsmag.com/
ENT: http://www.netline.com/ent/

Enterprise Systems Journal: http://www.netline.com/esj/
Government Computer News: http://www.netline.com/gn1/
HP Professional: http://www.netline.com/hpp/
ID Systems: http://www.idsystems.com/new.htm
Industry Report: http://www.industry.com/
InfoWorld: http://www.iwsubscribe.com/
Internet World: http://www.iwsubs.com/
Knowledge Management: http://www.sffaonline.com/sffan2/
subscribe/kmmag1.htm
LAN Times: http://www.netline.com/lt/
Microsoft Professional Magazine: http://www.mcpmag.com/
Midrange System: http://www.netline.com/mrs/
Network Magazine: http://www.networkmagazine.com/
subscribe/
Network World: http://www.nwfusion.com/subscribe.html
New Media: http://www.newmedia.com/subscribe/
Oracle Magazine: http://www.oramag.com/cgi-bin/oramag
Performance Computing: http://www.netline.com/urpc/
Sales and Field Force Automation: http://www.sffaonline.com/
sffan2/subscribe/sffa1.htm
Silicon India: http://www.siliconindia.com/subs.html
Smart Retailer: http://subscribe.smartreseller.com/
Software Development: http://www.sdmagazine.com/sdonline/
fr_subs.html
Software Magazine: http://www.netline.com/sm/
Solutions Integrator: http://www.sisubscribe.com/
Sun Expert: http://www.cpg.com/se/subscribe.html
Sun Express: http://www.netline.com/sunex/
Syllabus: http://www.syllabus.com/syllsub.html
Web Techniques: http://www.netline.com/webt/
Windows NT Systems: http://www.synasoft.com/hallmark/nt/
ntnew.html
Windows Pro Magazine: http://subscribe.windowspro.com/
Wings Web Guide: http://www.wingswebguide.com/freeform.
html

Free Clip Art and Graphics

#1 Clip Art: http://www.1clipart.com/
3D Animations: http://www.eclipsedigital.com/
Agriculture and Plants: http://desktoppub.about.com/cs/
freeclipartagri/
Clip Art Center: http://clipart.easyinteractive.com/
Clip World: http://www.totalclip-art.com/cgi-rank/out.cgi?cliprsc
Companion Software: http://maroon.com/cowboyclipart/
Cowboy Clip Art: http://maroon.com/cowboyclipart/
Food and Cooking Clip Art: http://desktoppub.about.com/cs/
freeclipartfood/
Free Clip Art: http://www.free-clip-art.com/
Free Web Graphics: http://desktoppub.about.com/library/gold/
blpics.htm
Gran Gran's Baby Software: http://home.att.net/~scorh/
GraphicsBaby.html
Holidays and Religion Clip Art: http://desktoppub.about.com/
cs/freeclipartholi/
Kid's Domain: http://www.kidsdomain.com/clip/index.html
Loving Hearts Designs: http://www.geocities.com/Heartland/
Prairie/2482/design10.html
People Clip Art: http://desktoppub.about.com/cs/freeclipart
people/
Total Clip Art: http://www.totalclipart.com/
True Free Clip Art: http://www.totalclipart.com/cgi-rank/
out.cgi?okbary
The Warehouse: http://www.iconcreation.com/warehouse.html
WebClipZ: http://www.webclipz.com/

Computer Accessories

Here are some businesses that provide a good assortment of computer accessories—cables, hard drives, keyboards, and more—at reasonable prices, often far less than you would pay at a local store. If you need something for your clients, check out these Web pages.

Allsop Computer Accessories: http://www.allsopcomputerstuff. com/

Astro Accessories: http://www.astrocomputer.com/Astro/ accat.htm

CinMar Promotions: http://www.cinmarpromotions.com/IBS/ SimpleCat/Shelf/ASP/Hierarchy/02.html

DataPro: http://www.cableco.com/

Dunning: http://www.dunning.net/

Grand Computer Accessories: http://www.grandcomponline. com/

HMNet Technologies: http://www.hmnettech.com/accessories. html

Laptop Computer Accessories: http://wirelessconnection.safe shopper.com/2/cat2.htm?10

MsEscher: http://www.worldofescher.com/store/compaccs.html

Northwest Computer Accessories: http://www.nwca.com/

Quality Accessories: http://www.inpace.com/

Quick Look Computer Accessories: http://www2.acan.net/ ~quick/

RJ Ross Computer Accessories: http://www.rjross.com

PAPER SOURCES

Baudville: http://www.baudville.com/

Donahue Paper: http://www.donahuepaper.com/

Greenleaf Paper Company: http://www.greenlinepaper.com/ quick.htm

Meijer: http://www.meijer.com/compsup/printer_paper.html

New Leaf Paper: http://www.newleafpaper.com/letterhead.html

Office Depot: http://www.officedepot.com/

Office Max: http://www.officemax.com/max/solutions/nav/ home.jsp

Paper Direct: http://www.paper-direct.com/

Queblo: http://www.ed-it.com/p_tcwe1.htm

Quill: http://www.quillcorp.com/

Free Software

a2B Music Player: http://www.a2bmusic.com/

AbiWord (word processing): http://www.abisource.com/dl_win32.phtml

Action Is (fonts): http://www.fontdiner.com/

Adobe Everywhere: http://www.adobe.com/products/acrobat/readstep.html

AdToOne (bulk e-mailer): http://www.zaisoft.com/

Anti-Virus Software: http://www.anti-trojan.net/

Anti-Virus Software: http://www.dosbin.com/antvir01.htm

Automatic Form Filler: http://service.bfast.com/bfast/click?bfmid=1307357&siteid=5663704&bfpage=1

Calendars: http://www.freewarefiles.com/results. php?categoryid=8&subcategoryid=80

Calendars and Clocks: http://www.dosbin.com/cal.htm

Casino Games: http://www.qksrv.net/click35119513158

Cdex (music files): http://www.softwarecenter.net/cdex/

Desktop Themes: http://www.freewarefiles.com/category/themes.htm

Desktop Utilities: http://www.completelyfreesoftware.com/index_all.html

E-Mail Monitoring: http://www.mailwasher.net/

E-Sword (Bible study): http://www.esword.net

Euduro (e-mail): http://www.eudora.com/

Fast Downloads: http://www.qksrv.net/click-35119-5593874

First Page (Web design): http://www.evrsoft.com/

The Free Bible: http://www.freebible.com/

Frequency Analyzer (voice analyzer): http://www.relisoft.com/

Games: http://www.freewarefiles.com/category/games.htm

Georgiat TrueType Fonts: http://www.microsoft.com/

Health and Nutrition: http://www.freewarefiles.com/results. php?categoryid=16&subcategoryid=175

Home Inventory: http://www.contactplus.com/products/freestuff/mystuff.htm

Internet Answering Machine: http://service.bfast.com/bfast/click?bfmid=32410730&siteid=35690826&bfpage=tl1

Internet Software: http://www.completelyfreesoftware.com/
internet_related_w31.html
Opera (Web browser): http://www.opera.com
ReadPlease (text-to-speech program): http://readplease.com/
RoughDraft (word processing): http://www.rsalsbury.co.uk/
roughdraft/
Screen Savers: http://www.jumbo.com/mm/ss/
Software Library (games): http://www.tucows.com/
Sphygmic (spreadsheet): http://www.sphygmic.com/sssheet.htm
Spirit of Australia (screen saver): http://www.kenduncan.com/
navframes/freetoys_index.htm
Star Office (word processing/spreadsheet/graphics): http://www.
sun.com/staroffice
Search Engine: http://answwwer.net/
Task Plus (calendar): http://www.freewarefiles.com/results.
php?categoryid=8&subcategoryid=80\
Ultimate Zip (file zipper): http://www.ultimatezip.com/
Video Games: http://ads.cpabank.com/serve/c.cfm?ad=564&aff=201
Virus Protection: http://www.vcatch.com/
Web Browser: http://www.amiweb.ca/
Work At Home: http://www.qksrv.net/click-35119-4010680
ZoneAlarm (firewall): http://www.zonelabs.com/CS/ home
office.html

FREE E-MAIL

If you'd like to use an e-mail address other than your present
one for business purposes, you can find a free one at any of these
sources.

Bigfoot: http://www.bigfoot.com/
Eudoramail: http://www.eudoramail.com/
Free E-Mail: http://www.emailaddresses.com/
Free E-Mail Guide: http://www.geocities.com/SiliconValley/
Vista/8015/free.html
Friendly E-Mail: http://www.friendlyemail.com/

Hotmail: http://lc2.law5.hotmail.passport.com/cgibin/login
Juno: http://www.juno.com/home_index3.shtml
My Own E-Mail: http://starmail.com
Topica: http://www.topica.com/
Yahoo Mail: http://mail.yahoo.com/